RAISED
IN SILENCE

LESSONS ON LISTENING, LOVE, AND LOUD FAMILY DINNERS FROM A CHILD OF DEAF ADULTS

MARIA GALLUCCI

Raised in Silence
Lessons on Listening, Love, and Loud Family
Dinners from a Child of Deaf Adults

Cover concept and image by Rian.
Cover design by Peaceful Profits.

Headshot photography by JC Buck.

Paperback ISBN: 978-1-967587-16-2
eBook ISBN: 978-1-967587-17-9

DISCLAIMER: Some names and identifying details in this book have been changed to protect the privacy of individuals and families. Certain events have been combined or adapted for narrative clarity. While every effort has been made to preserve the integrity of these stories, this memoir reflects one person's lived experience and perspective. Where applicable, facts about Deaf and Hard of Hearing culture have been reviewed for accuracy and shared with the intent to educate and promote understanding.

CODA /ˈKOʊ-DƏ/ (KOH-DUH) NOUN

Acronym for Child of Deaf Adults, referring to someone raised by one or more Deaf parents or caregivers. CODAs often serve as unofficial interpreters between the Deaf and Hard of Hearing community and the hearing world from a young age.

Praise for Maria Gallucci's *Raised in Silence:*
*Lessons on Listening, Love, and Loud Family
Dinners from a Child of Deaf Adults*

"A deeply personal glimpse into the experience of being Deaf. This book is a beautiful contribution to the conversation around identity, culture, and connection. I'm grateful for the space it creates to amplify diverse voices and lived truths."–Cliff Moers, former Director of Colorado Commission for the Deaf, Hard of Hearing, and DeafBlind

"Maria's story will change how you think about communication and what it means to show up for people on their terms. As someone who knows Maria from her success in the real estate world, she could have written about that. Instead, she wrote a deeply impactful book about being better to your fellow humans. *Raised in Silence* is an unforgettable reminder that being willing to meet other people where they are, even when their world looks different from yours, can unlock the most important connections in your life."–Robert Reffkin, founder and CEO of Compass

"This book is a treasure. A wonderful portrayal of Deaf culture and community experiences through the eyes of a CODA."–Sabrina, Director of Deaf Overcoming Violence through Empowerment (DOVE)

"American Sign Language is the transformative river that flows through the United States, engraving humanity's greatest gift into every generation. This book helps bridge that gap."–Jake Pfau-Martinez, President of Colorado Association of the Deaf

"This book sheds light on what it's like to be a hearing person growing up in the Deaf community and the unique challenges that can come with that."–Cody, CODA

"*Raised in Silence* is a quiet revelation. It's a tender, empathetic portrait of life within the Deaf and Hard of Hearing community, told with grace and clarity. It welcomes readers with open arms, offering deep inclusiveness without pretense, and reminds us to listen beyond words. A profoundly moving, human story that lingers with warmth and joy through hardship."–Mila, advocate

"Brava!! I applaud Maria for giving such a candid and intimate look into the life of a Deaf family and on growing up as a CODA. This is a beautiful and important book about love and resilience that everyone needs to read."–MT, philanthropist

"As a CODA with sign language as her first language, Maria is the perfect candidate to write about how people in the Deaf community struggle to navigate the hearing world in their daily lives. She has also served the Deaf community for years in her real estate business, which puts her in the perfect position to share her life experiences and those of the Deaf and Hard of Hearing community."–Anonymous

"Powerful, compassionate, and real, this book sheds light on what it truly means to belong in the Deaf community."–Melissa, Treasurer, Rocky Mountain Deaf School, Board of Directors and proud mother of a HoH/Deaf daughter

"Active listening and communication is critical in any relationship. Maria's book helps us apply those skills to better connect with those in the Deaf and Hard of Hearing community."–Heather Bustos, Regional Vice President for Compass

"Maria Gallucci is a rare force in this world. She is powerful in purpose, compassionate in presence, and deeply committed to making a meaningful impact through every word she writes in this amazing book!"–Skye Michiels, CEO of With Heart Coaching

"Powerful. Magnificent. Courageous."–John, retired from the Department of Defense, Air Reserve Personnel Center HQ

"Maria really becomes vulnerable as she shares her story in this book. While growing up, she didn't realize having Deaf parents was unique as it was her normal. In this beautiful book about home being family, Maria brings a special perspective to life as we know it in the stories she shares here. This is a must-read for anyone wanting to be part of and do right in promoting a more inclusive world."–Nadelle, Deaf adult and educator

For my dad, Ray "the Godfather"

My mom, Ellie

And my bonus mom, Dixie

Thank you for raising us to value kindness and connection. I'm proud to be part of a family that loves and celebrates others exactly as they are.

To the Deaf and Hard of Hearing community

Thank you for embracing those who feel different with open arms. You taught me what true acceptance looks like, and I'm forever grateful.

To other CODAs

Thank you for navigating two worlds with love and resilience. We grew up bridging gaps many never see. I see you, and your story matters.

To the hearing world

Thank you for deepening your understanding of the Deaf and Hard of Hearing community and what it means to connect with anyone who communicates differently. This is how we build a more compassionate world.

CONTENTS

INTRODUCTION

I was five years old when I saw a porta-potty fly across the sky. I watched from my bedroom window as the wind howled, trees blew sideways, and debris whipped through the air. Everything was loud, and there were all kinds of sounds I didn't recognize, but even my little kid brain knew something was wrong.

The problem: My mom couldn't hear the tornado sirens.

Eventually, she must have felt the house shaking. She looked up at the chaos outside, sprang into action, and rushed us downstairs to safety.

That was life as a Child of Deaf Adults (CODA). I learned early on that many things weren't designed with my parents in mind, like relying on sirens as a signal for danger. I had to start making sense of the world around me at a very young age in order to pick up on important details my parents might miss.

Like most CODAs, I fell into the role of interpreter before I even knew what that meant. It wasn't always easy, but it shaped the way I see *everything* and left me with plenty of stories to tell.

My Deaf Treasures

Most kids don't grow up interpreting for their parents during doctor's appointments, phone calls, or parent-teacher conferences. Most kids don't have strangers assume they're Deaf or Hard of Hearing (HoH) because they're signing with their family. Most kids don't realize before they've even started school that communication is so much more than words.

But for all the unique challenges in my life, I've had so many more gifts. Growing up, I felt like I didn't quite fit in anywhere, but the Deaf and HoH community embraced me without hesitation. They taught me we all speak the same language, even if we communicate differently. They showed me true acceptance and compassion—things the world could use much more of.

So now, I want to share those lessons and offer a glimpse into the culture, community, and communication that raised me. Whether you're Deaf or HoH, a CODA like me, or simply someone who wants to connect with others more thoughtfully, this book is for you.

When it comes down to it, we all want to be understood. Bridging communication gaps, through learning a new language or simply paying more attention, can make the world a brighter place for everyone.

What This Book Is

This book isn't just my story of growing up as a CODA. It's a labor of love, 15 years in the making, shaped and supported by the community I grew up in. My hope is that you'll come away with a deeper understanding of Deaf and Hard of Hearing culture, and you'll learn how we can *all* communicate with more awareness and empathy.

Inside, you'll find stories from my life, funny moments, lessons I've learned, and what it was like being a hearing child of Deaf parents. But you'll also hear from other voices in the community: Deaf and HoH friends, fellow CODAs, hearing spouses, and others who generously shared their experiences to help paint a fuller picture of what inclusion and connection really look like.

If you're hearing, you'll get practical insights for engaging with Deaf or HoH people in your life, whether that's a coworker, a neighbor, or someone you meet in passing. From useful American Sign Language (ASL) phrases to best practices for respectful communication, this book offers tools to bridge communication gaps that come up in your life.

For Deaf or HoH readers, I hope that this book provides valuable exploration of the culture, access to deeper connection, and supportive advocacy for this community I love so much. For CODAs, it's a reminder that you're not alone.

Ultimately, my goal is to make understanding easier so the Deaf and HoH and hearing worlds don't feel so separate. I've existed in both since the day I was born.

A Quick Map of the Book

I've broken this book into three parts:

- **Part 1: An Unheard Childhood:** What it was like growing up as a hearing child of Deaf parents, from navigating two cultures to becoming the family interpreter. These early stories explore communication, identity, and the power of presence in a household shaped by Deaf culture.

- **Part 2: The Universal Language of Love:** What it means to be truly understood at home, in hospitals, at work, and in love. This section explores how communication shapes our closest relationships and why presence, effort, and empathy matter more than perfect words.

- **Part 3: A More Inclusive World:** How to recognize communication barriers in everyday life, and take action to create spaces where everyone feels seen, supported, and included.

You don't need to know ASL or have Deaf or HoH family members to benefit from these pages. All you need is to be curious and willing to *just try* and connect with your fellow humans in a more meaningful way.

To connection,

Maria Gallucci

HOW TO READ THIS BOOK

Once when I was out shopping with my mom, she was blocking a doorway without realizing it.

"Excuse me."

"Excuse me."

"EXCUSE ME!"

The man behind her kept getting louder, but of course, my mom couldn't hear him.

He quickly grew annoyed, and I pulled my mom aside so he could leave.

This kind of thing happens all the time—little misunderstandings that could be avoided with more awareness of hearing loss and communication differences in general.

People generally aren't trying to be rude. They just don't know what they don't know. We move through life assuming people will pick up on the same cues we do, like hearing a siren, understanding the tone of a text message, or recognizing an unspoken social norm.

But not everyone experiences even the simplest messages the same way, and when everyone understands that, we all benefit.

That awareness helps us create a kinder, more inclusive world. That's exactly why I decided to write this book.

Communication Tip: Don't Make Assumptions

If someone doesn't react to you, don't assume negative intent.

They might be Deaf or HoH. They could be neurodivergent or process sensory input differently. It could simply be that they're having an off day. A little kindness goes a long way.

I've sprinkled insights like this throughout this book to encourage more understanding. You'll find communication tips, instructions for basic words and greetings in ASL, interesting facts about Deaf and HoH culture, and more.

At the end of each chapter, you'll see a summary of the biggest takeaways. I'll also offer prompts for deeper reflection, so you can explore how these concepts around communication, empathy, and inclusion show up in your life.

A Quick Guide to Terms in This Book

- **deaf** (lowercase d): Refers to the physical condition of hearing loss. This is often used in medical or clinical contexts.
- **Deaf** (capital D): Refers to the cultural identity of being Deaf. Deaf culture is as rich as any other with shared values, norms, traditions, and a primary language (like ASL).
- **HoH** (Hard of Hearing): Refers to people with partial hearing loss. In this book, you'll see it capitalized

when I mention the Deaf and HoH community. This community as a whole is sometimes referred to with the shorthand DHH.

- **CODA** (Child of Deaf Adults): Someone raised by one or more Deaf caregivers, like my siblings and me. CODAs often grow up bilingual and bicultural, navigating both Deaf and hearing worlds.

A Few Things to Keep in Mind

- **Pause and reflect.** If something challenges what you thought you knew, let it sink in. How does communication show up in your life? Who feels included in your world? Who might feel left out?
- **Share what you learn.** If a story resonates with you, start a conversation! Pass along an insight. The more we talk about communication differences, the easier they become to navigate.
- **Explore the resources.** At the back of this book, there's a glossary with more terms that I mention when discussing the Deaf and HoH community. You'll also find resources for communication and support, whether you're a member of this community or you want to find new ways to show up as an ally.

No matter why you picked up this book, I hope it stays with you long after the last page. I hope you'll carry the communication tools inside throughout your life, and pass them on to others along the way.

Part 1

AN UNHEARD CHILDHOOD

CHAPTER 1

WHEN YOUR NORMAL
ISN'T NORMAL

I was in kindergarten when I first realized my world wasn't quite like everyone else's. When you're little, you don't question your reality. Your home is your whole world and your family are the only people in it. The way you communicate with each other feels like the only way that exists. But as you get older and step outside your little bubble, you start to see that not everyone's world is like yours.

My first memory of having this realization was on a kindergarten class field trip to the Denver Zoo. My friend Christie and I sat under a tree waiting for our parents to pick us up. She started asking me questions about my mom, just the usual curious kid questions when something feels unfamiliar.

"Does she talk like us?" she asked.

I shrugged. "She talks with her hands."

That's when my mom showed up. She stepped out of the car, smiled, and waved, but instead of speaking, she started signing. For the first time, I was aware of my peers' reactions to my mom and me signing. They stared at us. Some of them whispered.

The staring from my classmates felt uncomfortable, more like my mom and I were an exhibit at the zoo rather than normal people just like them. I remember feeling something I didn't have words for at the time. Not embarrassment. Not shame. Just more awareness that this part of my life that felt so completely normal to me was...different.

From that moment on, other kids at school would often ask what it's like to have Deaf parents. My go-to response was: "Well, what's it like to have hearing parents?"

What Kids Can Teach Us

Some of my schoolmates' staring felt uncomfortable, more like my mom and I were an exhibit at the zoo rather than normal people just like them.

That's something I've seen over and over again, and not just as a kid, but as an adult, too. Adults hesitate around things they don't understand. That's something I've seen over and over again not only as a kid, but also as an adult. Sometimes they stay quiet. Other times, they make assumptions.

What I wish is that more people paired their curiosity with kindness, the way my friend Christie did, instead of letting uncertainty turn into fear or judgment. Kids have that curiosity naturally, and they don't hide their reactions. If they don't understand something, they don't pretend otherwise. But kindness can make the difference between Christie's questions, which felt like a friend trying to understand me, and the other children staring, which made me feel like I didn't belong.

My classmates weren't being mean when they asked questions about my parents; they were curious and maybe even confused. They'd never seen anyone communicate with their hands. When we don't have a frame of reference for something, our natural reaction is to pause and assess: *Is this normal? Should I know what's going on? How should I respond?*

But when we let uncertainty turn into avoidance, we miss opportunities to connect. Even if you don't know the right thing to say or do, bringing kindness and curiosity into your interactions can open the door for understanding and help someone feel seen.

Small gestures like learning a few basic signs, acknowledging someone with a friendly wave, or doing a little research on Deaf and HoH culture can be meaningful gateways to connection. It would have helped if more people around me had done that when I was growing up.

Learn ASL: "Nice to Meet You"

ASL is a fascinating language, but if you see someone signing, consider engaging rather than just watching. Knowing how to say "nice to meet you" is a great way to let a new Deaf or HoH acquaintance know that you're interested in connecting. Here's how to do it:

---

1. **Nice:** Place your left hand flat, palm up, with your fingertips facing out. Slide your flat right hand across it toward the person you're addressing.
2. **Meet:** Bring both pointer fingers up (like a "1" sign) and move them toward each other, like two people "meeting" in front of you.
3. **You:** Point forward toward the person you're addressing.

Loud Family Dinners

The smell of garlic and tomato sauce always lured my siblings and me back home after a Sunday playing outside. When we crashed through the front door, a giant pot of our mom's Sunday sauce bubbled on the stove, big enough to feed eight people. Next to it, pasta water rattled to a boil and meatballs sizzled in a skillet. Dad's favorite.

It was Spaghetti Sunday, our family's weekly tradition. (We're Italian, after all!)

My mom saw us out of the corner of her eye and waved to get our attention. When that didn't work, she yelled, "Bewaka!", her way of saying Maria.

I turned my head to look at her, and she signed the rest, "Tell your brothers and sisters to get cleaned up and come to the table. It's almost five o'clock."

I ran to her side, fished a few noodles out of the pot, blew on them, and then ran to flick one at Chris's face.

"Dinner time!" I shouted so the whole house could hear me. Chris washed his hands and within seconds, he'd landed another noodle right in the middle of my forehead.

"Hey!" I yelled, and just like that, the chase was on.

Mom continued setting the table like she didn't have a house full of children chasing each other with wet spaghetti, though I'm sure she felt our feet thundering back and forth. Just in time, Dad walked through the door from work.

Mom set down the last dish and hit it with her wooden spoon to get our attention. She signed with a grin: "The last one to the table has to give Dad their meatballs!"

Dad rubbed his belly and we all shrieked, racing to our chairs.

Growing up, we could get away with being much louder than other kids. My dad, Raymond "Ray" Gallucci, was born completely deaf due to a genetic condition. He never spoke or made noises. My mom, Eleanor "Ellie" Gallucci, became deaf at nine months old after her hearing was damaged from a combination of the measles and mumps. She was only able to hear loud noises, like a plane flying overhead, and she used her voice when necessary to keep us kids in line.

They met at an all-Deaf boarding school, got married two years later, and had six children. From oldest to youngest: Ben, Ursula (Urs), me, Chris, Melissa, and Rose. All of us are hearing, but ASL was the primary language we spoke at home.

Since my parents were Deaf, their perception of these dinners was silence. They saw a dining table surrounded by bodies in motion, fingers spelling out words, hands and faces communicating frustration or enthusiasm. Deaf culture shaped how we communicated with each other. Directness was valued, facial expressions carried as much meaning as words, and if you looked away while someone was signing, it was like hanging up on them when they're in the middle of a sentence. We had to rely on our sense of sight to "hear" our parents, and they had to do the same to "hear" us.

But for my siblings and me, loud was our normal. I've since learned that this is common among CODAs. We're often louder than other kids simply because we can get away with it. Friends loved visiting our "fun house," where you could yell across rooms and blast music because no one would tell you to keep it down.

Even communicating with our parents could be loud. At the dinner table that evening, Chris smacked the table to get Mom's attention. "Pass the meatballs, please," he signed, his little face and hands smeared with red sauce.

Just like most Sundays, Chris and Melissa giggled and played a made-up game with their food, Ben and Urs calmly ate their dinner, and I ate while feeding Rose, who was still a baby. Mom made sure we weren't making too much of a mess, and Dad watched the scene unfold with his usual half-smile.

These dinners didn't need to follow the rules of the outside world. The way we communicated worked for us. My parents didn't have to hear our laughter to know it was there, and we didn't have to hear our parents speak to feel their love. That's a universal truth I've carried with me throughout my life: Connection isn't about the way you communicate. It's about being present with the people around you.

As we grew older, we learned that the hearing world did have some different rules. Being as loud as we were as kids wouldn't fly outside of our house, and some of society's norms wouldn't work for us, either. In the hearing world, people spoke over their shoulders or shouted from the other room, while we had to make sure our parents could see our hands and faces. The hearing world relied on sounds like a doorbell ringing, while at my house, the lights flickered to indicate someone was at the door.

Communication Tip: Use Your Phone

If you need a quick way to communicate with someone who's Deaf or HoH when you can't use sign language, pull out your phone. Writing to each other back and forth in your notes app can help in a pinch.

There's also an app called Cardzilla that allows you to easily display messages in larger text for clear and quick communication even across distances. Visit the Resources Section at the back of this book for more communication tools.

The Man At the Door

When I was around six years old, a man pounded on our front door. My siblings and I looked up from where we were eating a snack at the kitchen table. Since my parents couldn't hear the frantic knocking, the three older siblings, Ben, Ursula, and me, approached the door and opened it slowly. In front of us stood a man who was dazed, injured, and covered in blood.

"I had an accident," he said, breathing heavily. "I crashed my motorcycle down the street. I didn't know where else to go."

He looked down at us three little children.

We just stood there, jaws probably on the floor, trying to make sense of what we were seeing. Then we did what any kid would. We ran to get our dad.

My dad helped the man inside, but he couldn't hear him describe what happened or the pain he was feeling.

"What hurts?" My dad signed.

I turned to the injured man. "Where are you hurt?"

"My ribs...my leg..." He gestured vaguely to his side.

I signed that to my dad. Dad asked another question. I interpreted it to the injured man. My siblings and I went back and forth like this until eventually, the man calmed down enough to call a friend to pick him up.

Even at six years old, I felt proud that I could help two people communicate. I could do something to help the adults in my world. I could speak between two people who otherwise wouldn't have understood each other at all.

Deaf and HoH Culture Insight: What Is Interpreting?

I use the word interpreting to describe how I helped my parents communicate with the hearing world. But let's be clear: I was not a professional interpreter then, and I'm not one now.

Professional interpreting between English and ASL is a highly skilled, trained profession that requires deep fluency in both languages, not only in words, but also in meaning, tone, and cultural context.

Interpreters follow a strict code of ethics, remain neutral, and are trained to handle sensitive, complex conversations in high-stakes situations from doctor visits to courtrooms. What I did as a kid was out of love and necessity, but it wasn't the same as what trained interpreters do.

Interpreting also isn't the same thing as translating.
- Interpreting: converting spoken or signed language in real time
- Translating: converting one written language to another

These are very different roles with different required skills. That's why it's a pet peeve for interpreters to be referred to as translators.

Trick-or-Treating: A Hidden Piece of CODA Communication

Not every situation is as urgent as the injured man at the door, but even the most ordinary childhood experiences like trick-or-treating came with an extra layer of awareness.

Most kids ran up to houses, rang the doorbell, and yelled, "trick or treat!" without a second thought. Their only concern was how much candy they could collect before bedtime.

My siblings and I went trick-or-treating, too, but as we walked through the neighborhood, we weren't just focused on stuffing our candy bags. We were making sure our family stayed safe, too.

We watched for passing cars to be sure my parents could see what they couldn't hear. We paid extra attention to people around us and let our parents know if a neighbor was trying to get their attention. If someone spoke to them in the dark, we could find ways to help interpret.

There were no lessons on how to interpret a casual conversation at the grocery store or step in when my parents needed help communicating at the doctor's office. These things were just part of our lives. We figured it out as we went. Kids are good at that.

I realize now that growing up as a CODA helped me develop communication skills that most kids don't develop until much later. I learned how to pay attention to facial expressions, body language, tone, and unspoken context.

These skills have helped me better support Deaf and HoH clients as a real estate agent. They've made me a more compassionate mother. And they've even helped me find more empathy for strangers. That's why these skills matter. Extending kindness and understanding to those whose lives differ from our own creates a more supportive world for everyone.

Learn ASL: More Than Gestures

ASL, one of many silent forms of communication, is as complex and expressive as spoken language. A common misconception is that ASL is a collection of gestures that mimic English words and phrases, but that couldn't be further from the truth. Signed languages have their own distinct grammar, syntax, and linguistic structure.

To show the difference from English, let's look at an example:

→ In English, we say: "Where are you going?"
→ In ASL, this is signed as: "You go where?"

ASL also uses nonmanual markers, like facial expressions to add meaning, almost like punctuation. For example, you could lower your eyebrows to indicate something you're signing is a question.

Finding My Place as a CODA

Realizing my world wasn't quite like everyone else's wasn't exactly an "aha" moment. It was more of a slow awareness that grew over time. And most kids come to that realization eventually. We all start out thinking that what happens inside the walls of our home is all there is until life shows us otherwise.

This realization looks different for everyone, and your "normal" can shift in meaningful ways over the course of your life. I once spoke with a parent of a Deaf+ daughter who said, "When my daughter was diagnosed with hearing loss, I realized our family experience wasn't going to match what I'd always assumed was normal."

Redefining your normal might mean acknowledging that life has taken a direction you didn't expect. There are changes and challenges along the way, but an unexpected path can also bring many unexpected gifts like new languages, new communities, and new ways of seeing the world.

Having Deaf parents gave me all of that and much more. Even when I was young, I *never* saw helping them navigate the world as a burden. It was just my life. And more than that, it's a gift I'm proud of. It connected me to a rich culture, deep friendships, and a community that's shaped the course of my life.

I'm proud that my parents raised me in a language that's so wonderfully expressive. I'm proud of the ways my childhood taught me to care for others. I'm proud that being bilingual gave me a deeper understanding of communication across different cultures.

I think that's a beautiful part of growing up, learning that while your differences may be challenging to navigate at times, they also give you unique opportunities to connect with the world.

Key Chapter Takeaways

- Everyone's normal is different. What's ordinary to you might be unfamiliar to someone else.
- People hesitate around what they don't understand. When you meet someone whose life is different from yours, curiosity is a better path than fear.
- ASL isn't simply hand gestures. It's a full language with its own grammar and structure.

Prompts for Deeper Reflection

1. Was there a time when you reacted to something unfamiliar with discomfort or fear? This is natural, so we likely all have at one time or another. How can you lean into curiosity next time?
2. Have you ever encountered someone whose communication style was different from yours? What went well? What might you do differently in the future?
3. Think of someone in your life who might feel different or left out. What's a small action you can take this week to help them feel more accepted?

CHAPTER 2

ADVENTURES OF A CHILD INTERPRETER

One of the first times I interpreted for my parents, I was barely tall enough to see over the principal's desk. Picture my mom and the principal looking down at tiny five-year-old Maria, pigtails, Velcro shoes, and all, as I bounced back and forth between English and ASL to sign myself up for kindergarten.

I did my best to explain documents and answer the principal's questions. But let's be honest, I was far more concerned about when I'd get to play on the playground than I was about understanding the school's registration policies. Still, I got used to the grown-up situations quickly. By the time I was six or seven, I was taking phone calls, receiving packages at the door, and, when needed, even helping pay the bills.

This was our normal growing up. We didn't know any different. The only time I remember feeling stressed about helping my parents was when people stared, or when they were treated unfairly because they were Deaf. The hardship came not from their deafness, but from the world around us.

Being the family interpreter was just one part of the job. Ben, Urs, and I (the older siblings) became mini-parents in a way, and we helped raise our younger brothers and sisters. In addition to interpreting out in the world, we took care of the babies when they cried, or we ran to Mom or Dad signing to let them know that one of the little ones needed attention.

None of this felt like a burden to me, it was just my life. Plenty of kids take on extra responsibilities to support their families from a young age, whether it's helping in a family business, caring for younger siblings, or speaking for family members with communication differences. But it did mean I knew a lot more about finances, mortgages, and paying bills than any of my friends!

Deaf and HoH Culture Insight: Visual Cues

In a Deaf or HoH household, doorbells and phones don't ring. They flash! When someone called our landline or rang the doorbell in our house growing up, the lights would flicker to let us know.

My CODA friend, Andrew, said his flickering doorbell scared his childhood friends at first. They thought the house must be haunted when someone came to the door and suddenly, all of the lights flashed off and on.

Learning to Speak in a World That Didn't Speak Like Me

Since ASL is my first language, English is technically my second. But I didn't learn it like most bilingual kids would. When we older siblings were still little, we didn't have spoken

English conversations at home to reinforce the language. Bedtime stories were not read out loud. So, we started learning English by watching TV. We mimicked speech patterns from cartoons and sitcoms, but most of our communication was in ASL until we started going to school. Because of that, I always felt behind in English classes.

In second grade, I proudly turned in a writing assignment only for my teacher to circle an entire sentence in red ink and write "What?" above it. I had written "We go store after school." That structure would be fine in ASL, so I was confused. Wasn't it clear what I meant?

At first, I didn't think much about my communication. I never struggled to get my point across with my family at home. But at school, my siblings and I didn't always speak like the other kids, which affected everything from our communication to our social lives.

Even though we were pros at helping our parents with grown-up conversations, we had a harder time developing social skills than the other kids. That alone gave me intense anxiety, but then I found myself being excused from class to attend speech therapy.

> ### Fun Fact: In Some Ways, ASL Is Like Spanish
>
> If you've ever learned Spanish, you know that some phrases seem "backward" compared to their English equivalent. ASL is similar to Spanish in that way.
>
> For example, in English, we say **grilled cheese,** but in ASL, the word order flips, so we sign it as **cheese grill.**
>
> That's how Spanish is, too. For example, in English, we say **red car,** but in Spanish, it's **car red** (coche rojo).
>
> ASL isn't just English in a different order. It's a *conceptual language.* That means it's built around ideas, not direct word-for-word translations. For example, there are many different signs for English words like "run" or "fall," depending on the context. Think about how you could be "running" a race, "running" for office, or your nose might be "running." That's why it's so important to understand meaning rather than just memorizing vocabulary words.
>
> So remember, if you're learning ASL, try to avoid translating word-for-word from English in your head. Think of it as its own language, like Spanish.

Bilingual Kids in Speech Therapy

Everyone has struggles and insecurities. My parents struggled to communicate because they were Deaf, and I struggled to communicate because I stuttered. My parents' struggles were worse than mine, but I can empathize. I was teased for my communication differences. I struggled to get words out smoothly and felt frustrated when my thoughts came faster than my mouth could keep up. That didn't happen when I was signing.

That's why Ben, Urs, and I wound up in speech therapy. I was pulled out of class for the sessions, which made me feel even more like an outcast. I sat in a quiet room practicing sounds, repeating words, and trying to make this communication method flow as naturally as my ASL. It was strange being fluent in two languages, yet still needing to "fix" how I communicated to fit in better with the world around me.

This experience made me even more aware of how communication is judged not only by what you say but also by how you say it. I knew another CODA who had to go to speech therapy because he "sounded Deaf." He had learned English primarily from his Deaf parents and picked up on their unique speech patterns.

My sister, Urs, is another example. She didn't speak until she was a lot older than when the typical child starts talking. She's 18 months older than me, but for a long time, I was responsible for speaking for her. We did speech therapy together sometimes to help her get comfortable speaking around people outside of our family.

Looking back, I know I was lucky to have access to speech therapy. But I also wish there had been more awareness that *different* doesn't mean *wrong*.

CODAs, like me and many other bilingual kids, grow up constantly switching between languages, adapting to different communication styles, and thinking in more than one linguistic structure. Wouldn't it be cool if the adults in their lives acknowledged and celebrated those unique skills, rather than seeing them as something to fix?

But communication differences weren't always limiting for me. I had my own sneaky ways of using my skills to my advantage.

Communication Tip: How to Support CODA Kids

Teachers: Be patient with their English skills. ASL and English have different structures. Offer extra support with reading and writing. If a CODA student is struggling, find the skill they love practicing most and nurture it.

Friends: Don't stare when people use sign language. Try asking respectful questions about their experience as a CODA, and learn a few signs so you can communicate with their parents.

Parents: Encourage CODAs to set boundaries and meet other CODAs if they can. Celebrate your kid's bilingual skills, and help them explore other strengths as well.

Getting Away with (Almost) Anything

There were certainly some moments at school where I felt a little jealous of hearing families. Parent-teacher conferences stand out among them. I'd watch other kids off to the side, doodling or playing while their parents laughed with the teacher. It all seemed so easy. Meanwhile, I had to be on alert to interpret the entire exchange.

But there are some benefits to being the intermediary between your parents and your teacher, I discovered that I had some power over how these conversations went. If the teacher said "Maria talks too much in class," I could easily adjust that to "Maria is very social and makes lots of friends."

I wasn't necessarily *lying*…just doing a bit of light editing on the fly!

One time during a parent-teacher conference, my teacher sighed and said "Maria has a habit of passing notes when she should be paying attention."

I turned to my parents and signed, "Maria is very expressive and loves communicating with her classmates."

My mom nodded approvingly. "That's good," she signed back. "She's social, just like me."

My teacher, of course, had no idea what I had just said.

I sat there, feeling proud that I had gotten away with it. That is, until my dad, who could always read my face better than anyone, raised an eyebrow and signed "Tell me exactly what she said." Busted.

My siblings and I enjoyed testing how much we could get away with, especially during our birthday week. Three of our birthdays fall back-to-back in early June (mine on the 9th, Chris on the 8th, and Rose on the 7th), so we threw a giant party every year. Friends came over to swim, eat cake, and spend the night. It was total chaos.

Chad, one of Chris's childhood friends, recently reminded me just how loud those summer birthday parties were compared to anything he was used to. We'd scream, cannonball into the pool, and play our music as loud as it would go because our parents couldn't hear us. Unfortunately, our neighbors could. Every year, like clockwork, they'd come over to complain about the noise.

Chris and Chad would occasionally push the boundaries further, too. They'd ride their bikes out to the country store to get 25 cent packs of Garbage Pail Kids cards, sticks of gum, and those little beef jerky cans of chew. They were often gone way too long and when they realized the time, they'd fly back home on their bikes and try to play it off like they'd been there all along. But Mom and Dad *always* noticed. They'd yell at Chris, mom with her voice, and both of them in ASL.

Sometimes I wonder what our childhood would've been like if our parents were hearing. Would we have gotten in more trouble? Would we have been disciplined more strictly? I thought about what it'd be like if Dad were to yell at us, knowing how other kids my age would freeze when their dads raised their voices. I just couldn't picture it. My dad's anger never rose in volume. It would come in stern looks and rapid signs that you could almost feel flying through the air.

You could never underestimate my parents' ability to pick up on cues beyond sound. They might not have heard the door creak open or the teacher's exact words, but they could read our faces. Growing up in a Deaf household didn't mean we got away with everything. We did get creative, but even then, we rarely fooled them for long.

> **Communication Tip: Use Emojis to Clarify Tone**
>
> Something I always tell hearing people when communicating with my Deaf or HoH clients and friends is that tone can be hard to pick up on, even in writing.
>
> Everyone is different, but to some people with communication differences, the average person texts in a way that can feel more blunt or harsh than intended. The tone of a written message can be tricky to interpret without body language or facial expressions to follow.
>
> One way you can clarify the tone you want to convey in a message is to use plenty of emojis. For example, if I was texting you the story above, I'd end my message with the crying-laughing emoji to indicate that it was meant to be funny.

Finding Where I Fit in the World

For my siblings and me, being CODAs was our normal. But on the harder days, I felt like my purpose in life was to be an interpreter rather than a normal child.

Other CODAs I know have shared similar feelings. My friend Nadelle is Deaf, and her sons, Cody and Austyn, told me there were plenty of times they had to interpret things that were way too grown up for their age. But they also felt proud that they could understand those complex ideas at such a young age and help their mom understand them too.

Unfortunately, I didn't have CODA friends I could connect with on these things growing up. While my dad used to tell me that having a few good friends was enough, I longed to fit in with the cool kids at school. Some classmates thought it was cool that my parents and I communicated with sign language, but others made fun of me for being different.

At home, my hands flew through conversations. At school, I sometimes hesitated before speaking, worried about being judged. I loved my family's language and culture, but I also craved the easy acceptance of my peers. Sometimes, I felt like I didn't fully fit in anywhere.

That tension isn't unique to me. Another CODA I know, Claudia, shared her experience navigating the complicated emotions that those in-between spaces can kick up.

"My mother always thought I was embarrassed of her deafness," Claudia told me. "When we went to school functions, I couldn't walk away from her to talk to my friends. If I did, she'd tell me later that I must have done that because I was embarrassed of her."

Of course, Claudia was just being a kid. Even when she was young, she was always proud of her mom. But I can understand why her mom took it to heart. When you've spent your life feeling like the world wasn't built for you, even small things can feel like proof that you don't belong, whether or not that was anyone's intent.

The truth is that Claudia's friends thought it was so cool that she could sign and always wanted to learn from her. Even the troublemakers thought her life was cool because she could blast her stereo as loud as she wanted without her mom telling her to turn the music down.

CODAs learn so much about communication from a young age. We learn empathy and how to see things from other people's perspectives, which are strengths for me now as an adult. Being a CODA made me a natural caregiver, and those skills have served me as a parent, friend, and even as a real estate agent.

For people who didn't navigate communication differences growing up, know that taking the time to understand what it's like will have a ripple effect in people's lives. When you show up with empathy, you become someone who feels safe to be around, even if you don't speak the same language.

Key Chapter Takeaways

- CODAs grow up balancing at least two languages. For American CODAs like me, that's ASL and English. This can affect how we communicate.
- Interpreting for parents at a young age builds independence, but can also make young kids feel self-conscious.
- Deafness and other communication differences can affect how someone interprets tone. Use emojis to help people understand the tone of your written messages.

Prompts for Deeper Reflection

1. Have you ever had to interpret or explain something between two people who couldn't understand each other? How did it feel? What would it be like to have to do that all the time?
2. What would you do if you met a child whose communication style differed from yours? Could you still connect through other means like art or music?
3. What's one small thing you can do to make communication easier for someone in a different language or culture?

CHAPTER 3

GROWING UP FAST

Purchasing property can be stressful for anyone. But imagine doing it when you can't hear the lender discussing loan options or the real estate agent explaining market trends and closing costs. Now imagine having to rely on your *child* to accurately interpret those details to you. (No pressure, little Maria!)

Most real estate agents don't get their start before they're ten years old, but that's basically what happened to me. Still in elementary school, I found myself talking to mortgage lenders, helping my parents gather paperwork, and interpreting all of the conversations that go into buying a new house.

My feet couldn't even touch the floor but there I was, sitting between my parents at the kitchen table, paperwork spread out in front of us, listening to the lender's questions over the phone.

"They need your financial statements," I signed to my parents, making sure we collected the right materials to bring to our meeting.

"Ask him if this will affect our monthly payments," Mom signed to me, then I did my best to form those big words to the man on the phone.

By the time we were picking paint colors for the new house, I understood and could explain in two languages concepts like interest, lending, and fixed-rate mortgage. Meanwhile, other kids my age were practicing cartwheels and secret handshakes on the playground.

I knew I was meeting with people who seemed important, but it didn't feel out of the ordinary to me. I was constantly being pulled into grown-up conversations to interpret everything from checkups at the dentist to explaining problems to the plumber. I went back and forth between English and ASL like it was no big deal, even though I was still in elementary school and had only just learned to read chapter books.

Looking back now, I can only imagine what the adults in all those interactions must've thought when I helped my parents buy their house. Maybe they were confused or impressed watching this little kid communicate big words like *deductible* in two languages without flinching. But I didn't know any different. To me, it was just another Tuesday.

Fun Fact: How Do Phone Calls Work?

When I was growing up, we had this machine called a TTY (teletypewriter). Tell me I'm not the only one who remembers these!

It was a clunky device that connected to a phone line so you could type back and forth instead of speaking. You'd type out your message, and it would appear on the other person's TTY screen. This machine only let you call other Deaf people or people who owned TTYs. Some businesses had TTYs, but they were often off or in an office with someone who didn't know how to use them.

Interestingly, many businesses still have a TTY line listed even though most hearing employees haven't touched one in years. If you asked them how to use it today, you'd probably get a blank stare.

Technology has come a long way since then. Now, Deaf and HoH people use video phones (VP) and Video Relay Services (VRS), which allow them to communicate in ASL even if they need to speak with someone who doesn't know the language.

With VRS, a professional ASL interpreter joins a live video call to relay messages between the Deaf caller (who signs in ASL) and the hearing person (who speaks on a regular phone). It's like having a live interpreter in the middle of your phone call, but all done virtually.

Childhood, Accelerated (Again)

For the most part, I was comfortable in my role as a tiny grown up who helped my parents move through their life. I felt a deep determination to protect them and ensure they weren't mistreated. From helping them navigate home buying to acting as a mini-parent to my younger siblings, caring for others has always been a natural instinct for me.

That's why I felt more prepared than other teenagers might have felt when I found out I was pregnant at 15.

Like most people with anything slightly "different" about them, I already felt like an outsider in high school. The bullying had gotten worse, and I didn't exactly fit into any social group. Then add a pregnant belly hiding underneath my schoolbooks and needless to say, I didn't have a good time in high school.

When I became a mother to my beautiful daughter, Jordan, I was suddenly so much more than a child of Deaf adults. I was a parent, too. In some ways, it felt like a continuation of the life I was already living, taking care of others and making decisions most kids my age didn't have to think about.

It's not like I had been going to parties or dances before. I was usually busy helping my family. I wasn't the kid who snuck off to football games on Friday nights. I was the one interpreting why the water heater wasn't working between my dad and the plumber in the kitchen.

I finished high school as quickly as possible. By 16, I had graduated early, moved into my own place as a single mom, and started working to provide for my new little one.

My parents were supportive in the ways they could be, but I think they were worried initially. They knew how hard life already was for me, and they knew this would make it harder. But they also trusted me. They watched me step up again and again, and they believed I would find a way to take care of Jordan just like I'd always taken care of my family.

My parents were supportive, but I was determined to be as independent as I could. I paid my mom to babysit while I worked, and she communicated with Jordan in sign language, just as she had with my siblings and me.

One evening after work, I came home drained, juggling grocery bags in my new professional work clothes. Jordan sat on the floor waving her arms and looking up at my mom with bright eyes. She concentrated hard as her little fingers moved through the air.

"She has something to show you," my mom signed with a smile.

I knelt down, and then Jordan did it. Her tiny hand formed the sign for "I love you," all on her own for the very first time.

My knees hit the floor. I didn't know whether to laugh or cry, so I did a bit of both. Somehow through the weight of bills and the exhaustion from work, I was doing it. That little sign from Jordan told me everything I needed to hear: *You're doing okay. I feel safe. I feel loved.*

Everything came full circle at that moment. Any doubt I had that I was strong enough to handle motherhood at such a young age disappeared. Just 16 years earlier, my mom had taught me to sign "I love you," and now my daughter was signing it back to me in my first language, the perfect reminder that no matter what, we've got each other.

Fun Fact: Teaching Sign Language to Babies

Did you know that babies can learn to communicate with hand signs before they speak? Research shows that signing helps reduce frustration in babies and young children by allowing them to express their needs earlier than they can through spoken words.

Simple signs like "milk," "more," "eat," and "all done" can give babies a way to communicate before they develop verbal skills. Plus, signing strengthens parent-child bonding, something I experienced firsthand with Jordan.[1]

CODA Mischief

The phone rang on my bedside table and I jolted awake.

"Hello?" I asked in a raspy, half-asleep voice.

"Yes, is this Rose's mom?"

I sat up in bed. *Oh no, what has Rose gotten into?*

I was used to protecting my siblings, so I got the memo. Time to put on my best mom voice. "Yes, I'm Rose's mom. Who am I speaking with?"

"This is Officer Sherman with the county sheriff's department. We found Rose out past curfew on the church property. There were several kids on four-wheelers. Did you know your daughter was out tonight?"

---

1 Susan W. Goodwyn and Linda P. Acredolo, "Impact of Symbolic Gesturing on Early Language Development," *Journal of Nonverbal Behavior* 24, no. 2 (2000): 81–103, https://www.researchgate.net/publication/226583485_Impact_of_Symbolic_Gesturing_on_Early_Language_Development.

I paused dramatically, as any concerned mother would.

"Yes, Officer, I'm aware she was out there," I said, trying to lower my voice and sound very maternal. "We talked about it earlier. Is everything okay?"

He was quiet for a second. I could practically hear him squinting through the phone.

"She's fine, but…you gave her permission to be out there?"

"Yes, I did," I said firmly. "She knows to be safe, and I trust her judgment. But thank you for calling. I appreciate you checking in."

"All right then," he said, clearly surprised. "Well…thank you for your cooperation. She'll be home soon."

"Of course. Have a good night, Officer."

All of the other kids who got caught that night were grounded. Rose, on the other hand, walked away with a smirk, because her "mom" had given her permission.

As I mentioned in chapter 2, growing up in a Deaf household sometimes meant we could get away with more than our friends, and we knew it. While I was busy raising Jordan as a teen, my siblings enjoyed the perks of being teenage CODAs. They were able to sneak out without getting caught because my parents couldn't hear them tiptoeing down the stairs or out the creaky front door.But our family dynamic wasn't always about pushing boundaries for fun. I grew up with a strong pull to protect my siblings, and I'm glad Rose knew she could lean on me for support, even if that meant bending the rules a little from time to time!

At the end of the day, I love the way we grew up. The role I played in my family was different and I had more responsibilities than my peers. Sometimes I had to show up as a protector and a parental figure for my siblings. But our home was always full of love, laughter, and this constant sense of "we've got each other." Even when signing in public drew stares, kids mocked our parents' voices, or people treated us like we were weird, we stuck together.

My siblings and I were the only unofficial "kid interpreters" we knew. While that felt lonely at times, the close-knit support system we developed between us from that shared experience is still there today, and I wouldn't have it any other way.

Deaf and HoH Culture Insight:
Representation Matters

Have you ever seen a kid light up and say, "That's me!" when they see a character they relate to on TV? Seeing people who speak your language or share your life experiences in movies, books, or on TV can make you feel like you belong.

That's why representation in the media is so important. It's pretty rare for Deaf or HoH and CODA kids, so it was exciting when the 2021 film *CODA* came out. It has Deaf actors using ASL and tells the story of a hearing daughter of Deaf parents. The main character's story is similar to mine, so I finally have a movie I can point to and say, "That was my childhood!"

I recommend watching it and exposing yourself to more media about people with different backgrounds than your own. When we take time to learn stories outside our experience, we move toward a more understanding and supportive world.

Who Are You Outside of Your Roles?

For CODAs and anyone who has spent their life in a caretaker or supportive role, it can be easy to let those roles become your identity. But who are you outside of that?

When your identity is built entirely around caring for others, it's easy to lose sight of your own needs, passions, and purpose. Over time, you may start to feel as if your worth comes from what you do, not who you are.

As a CODA and then a young, single mother, my identity was based on supporting others from an early age. But in adulthood, my real estate career became an empowering outlet. It allowed me to take control of my future, while still supporting the Deaf and HoH community I love so much.

It might be something completely different for you. The idea is to give yourself a little space to remember that you're more than what you do for others.

Take a moment to reflect on who you are beyond the roles you play.

Step 1: Write Out Your Roles

Grab a pen and paper and list out the roles you play in life. Think about:

- Family: sibling, child, parent
- Work or education: student, lawyer, builder
- Daily responsibilities: hard worker, problem solver, creative thinker

Step 2: List Your Hobbies and Dreams

Now, let's think about what makes you *you* outside of the roles you identified. Maybe you're:

- An aspiring marathon runner
- An avid reader
- A weekend gardener

Think back to your childhood too. What did you love doing the most?

Now let's look forward. What are your biggest, wildest dreams? How do you feel? What are you doing? Who are you with? Capture as much as you can.

Step 3: Bridge the Gap

Look at both lists. Consider how much of your life is spent serving others, and how much is spent on things that bring you joy. Are there small ways you can make more space for yourself?

Growing up fast wasn't something I chose, but something life asked of me again and again. From interpreting mortgage terms in elementary school to becoming a teenage mom, I learned how to take care of others before ever learning how to take care of myself.

While I'm grateful for the strength, grit, and love that shaped me, I'm still learning who I am beyond the helper role that's been part of me for as long as I can remember. In some ways, I think that's what we're all here to do: find gratitude for the identities life gives us, and discover the depths of who we are *beyond* those roles too.

Key Chapter Takeaways

- CODAs take on adult roles like interpreting, caregiving, and advocating for their families from a young age.
- Deaf and HoH households operate differently, which can give CODA kids unique freedoms, challenges, and independence.
- Navigating adult responsibilities early can prepare you for challenges down the road. But it's also essential to discover who you are beyond the roles you've always played.

Prompts for Deeper Reflection

1. Do you know any children or young adults who had to grow up faster than their peers? Is there anything you can do to support them, even if it's just kicking a ball around for an hour so they feel like a kid again?
2. Think about a time when your environment gave you freedom or held you back. How did it affect the choices you made?
3. In what ways do you define yourself by the roles you play for others? What parts of your identity exist outside of those roles, and how can you nurture them?

Part 2

THE UNIVERSAL LANGUAGE OF LOVE

CHAPTER 4

HARD CONVERSATIONS
MADE HARDER

Nothing could have prepared me for the day I had to sign to my parents: "The doctor says there's nothing more they can do."

My mom had melanoma in her thirties. She beat it then, and we thought that chapter was behind us. But almost a decade later in late 2000, she started complaining about a nagging pain in her right shoulder. At first, she brushed it off, thinking she might have just slept funny. But the pain got worse. She said she felt it deep in her shoulder, as if it went right to the bone. Then she started having trouble lifting her arm, so we went to the doctor.

He said she needed rotator cuff surgery. As soon as those words left the doctor's lips, I knew something was off. One of us kids had been there for all of our parents' doctor appointments since we were little. We all knew Mom's medical history by heart. That just didn't add up.

Rotator cuff surgery is common among athletes and people with physically demanding jobs. My mom lived with epilepsy since she was young, so she hadn't played sports a day in her life. She was a stay-at-home mom with no past shoulder injuries. She was still relatively young, so age-related wear and tear didn't make sense either.

I couldn't shake the feeling that we were missing something, so I took a deep breath and forced out the one question I never wanted to have to ask: "Has anyone checked to see if her cancer is back?"

They hadn't. The doctor agreed to schedule a PET scan, and within the week, we were already back in the doctor's waiting room for a third time to get the results.

There were rarely ASL interpreters available to attend appointments with us back then, so my siblings and I would coordinate to make sure someone could be at every appointment. I went to this one, too, to help my parents communicate and make sure we got the answers we needed. The clinic was busy that day—phones ringing, nurses calling out names from behind the front desk, and the constant movement of patients coming and going.

When my mom's name was called, I gave her a nudge and we all stood up together, tense with worry, shoes squeaking on the floor tiles in unison until we arrived at a small room. Mom sat on the exam table, Dad sat on the extra chair meant for family, and I leaned against the wall, running through everything I might need to ask, but trying to look calm.

As soon as the doctor came back into the room, I knew it was bad. I could tell by the look on her face. The doctor said my mom's cancer was back, and it was everywhere. There was nothing they could do.

Before I could process any of this, I had to be the one to break the news to my parents. I signed to them everything the doctor had said, and my heart sank as I watched their expressions fall. Dad's eyes narrowed. Mom's shoulders slumped.

Several seconds passed with no noise. No moving hands. In a Deaf family, silence and stillness are one and the same. It felt like all of the oxygen had left the room, but somehow I had to breathe anyway.

"Hey. Hey!" I shook my hand to pull my parents back into the present moment with me.

"It'll be okay," I signed, even though we all knew it wouldn't. What else do you say in a moment like that?

I wasn't just delivering news. I was delivering a devastating blow to our family, and I couldn't even react to the emotion welling up inside of me. I was still the conduit between them and the doctors, so I had to stay composed enough to understand and communicate our next steps.

From there, everything moved fast. Hospice. Paperwork. Pain management.

My sister Melissa did most of the daily caregiving. She took off work so she could focus on keeping Mom as comfortable as possible. She managed the medications, helped her bathe as the pain grew worse, and adjusted pillows when Mom couldn't get herself out of bed. I handled the conversations with doctors, filled out endless forms, and sent updates to family and friends who wanted to know how things were going.

I also stepped in to make sure my youngest sister Rose, who was only 17 and a junior in high school at the time, maintained as many of her routines as possible. I did my best to help her with things like math homework and meals. I didn't know it then, but one day Rose would be in the same position I was, forced to sign devastating news from a doctor to one of our parents.

The six of us siblings each played our role in those final weeks of our mom's life. None of us were prepared, but somehow, we all just stepped in.

Mom said she wanted to stay alive long enough to watch the Denver Broncos play one last game, and she did. We watched it together at home as one last family activity.

Mom passed away shortly after that, in January 2001, just two and a half months after we found out her cancer was back.

Telling my parents about my mom's cancer wasn't just the hardest thing I've ever had to do. It was also a reminder of how much Deaf and HoH people still have to fight for basic communication and care. We didn't have anyone to help us navigate any of this. It was just us kids doing our best to explain impossible things to the people we loved most.

Years later, I still think about how much it would have helped if there had been anyone other than me who could speak both languages in the room with us when we got the news. Someone trained and neutral could've removed those barriers and responsibilities. I could have just been a daughter, and Mom could have been a patient with the same communication access as anyone else.

Deaf and HoH Culture Insight: How Do Doctor's Appointments Work?

For many Deaf and HoH patients, medical appointments are an uphill battle. Interpreters aren't always available, and video remote interpreting (VRI) services, where an interpreter attends the appointment live via video call, are only a recent development.

When they are available, they can be unreliable, lagging or cutting out at the worst moments. Also, sometimes the Deaf person is expected to stand up or sit at a weird angle to see the screen. They may even have to hold the screen because there's no stand for it. How can they communicate with their hands if they're busy holding the device?

Without in-person or reliable remote interpretation, Deaf and HoH adults still rely on their children, friends, or untrained staff to interpret deeply personal, high-stakes information.

- Family members bear the responsibility of interpretation.
- Doctors could fail to notice something important.
- Patients could miss critical details.
- Privacy is lost.

Imagine having to talk about your sexual health, terminal illness, or mental health struggles through your child. Now imagine being that child.

If you work in healthcare or support someone who is Deaf or HoH, here's how to help:

- Ask if an interpreter is needed. Don't assume.
- Advocate for in-person interpreting whenever possible.
- Don't rely on family members to interpret unless it's an emergency.
- Ensure VRI systems work and staff are trained to support Deaf and HoH patients.

What's Changed and What Hasn't

In 2019, almost 20 years after my mom passed, my dad developed melanoma too. This allowed me to see firsthand how far accommodations for Deaf and HoH patients have come in that time, and the ways they're still limited.

The hospital had VRI available this time and, supposedly, better protocols in place. But you'd be surprised how often those tools still let us down. The video would lag or freeze, and sometimes the picture was too blurry to see the interpreter clearly. During one appointment, Dad squinted at the monitor when the interpreter signed something, then he waved it off and signed to me, "Forget it, I'll just guess. They're probably saying I owe them money."

He always found a way to lighten the moment, but he was rightfully frustrated that he couldn't access important messages about his health, even when the messages were right in front of him. After everything Mom went through and all the time that had passed since her death, he still needed his kids to help him communicate through his own cancer journey.

Rose was still in school when our mom got sick, but she was able to attend more appointments with Dad as an adult. She could focus on simply being there for him when the video relay system worked, but often she had to step in and interpret like I did for Mom.

At one appointment, the doctor shared devastating news that Rose hoped she wouldn't have to deliver herself. But the VRI screen froze, and suddenly it was up to her to sign the same words I'd signed to my parents decades earlier: "Dad, they said there's nothing else they can do."

I wish I could have protected Rose from having that same heartbreaking experience. I wish the interpretation services could have taken that responsibility off her shoulders. But history managed to repeat itself.

When my dad passed away in November 2022, the world still hadn't caught up to the consistent, reliable accommodations the Deaf and HoH community deserves. I'd like to see that change in my lifetime. Families like mine are used to making it work, but we all deserve comfortable health appointments, accurate details on what's happening with our bodies, and space to just be present with our families.

Rightful Frustration

Even now, the frustration hasn't disappeared. I hear it all the time from friends in the community. Just recently, my friend

Melanie texted me to vent about her experience as a Deaf patient at her local clinic.

"I'm SO annoyed right now. I've waited an hour for my appointment and several hearing people have been seen ahead of me. They know I'm Deaf and I booked the appointment weeks ago."

I felt frustrated for Melanie and frustrated at how familiar this experience was.

Twenty minutes later, she sent an update.

"They just brought me to an examination room, but they're still not talking to me. They're struggling to get the VRI system to work. This isn't the '90s anymore. Why haven't these problems been solved yet? Can't they just get an in-person interpreter?!"

I think sometimes hearing people, even well-meaning ones, expect Deaf and HoH people to be endlessly patient. To sit, wait, and be grateful for whatever scraps of access are offered. But that's not only an unfair expectation, it's also exhausting to wait in silence while people figure out how to behave around you.

Even systems designed with good intentions can be frustrating for everyone involved. I wanted to hear what these situations can look like from the provider's side, so I asked a healthcare professional I know, Amy, to share her experience.

"We rely on video interpreters to communicate with Deaf and HoH patients." Amy explained that in addition to the reliability of the technology, other challenges can come up, too.

"If a patient is elderly, they may have a hard time seeing the interpreters on the screen. Also, some patients prefer family to interpret, but family isn't always available, or they can accidentally misinterpret something important."

That's another important point: CODAs, like my siblings and I, aren't medical interpreters. Just because we're bilingual in sign language doesn't mean things won't get lost in translation. The Deaf and HoH community shouldn't *need* to rely on hit-and-miss communication for access to basic care.

What It Comes Down to

Things have come a long way since my mom's terminal diagnosis, but many systems still aren't built with the Deaf and HoH community in mind. We all deserve to be considered. We all deserve to feel understood. None of us should be expected to be flexible, wait longer, or make it work, while everyone else gets to move through the world without the same communication barriers.

Unfortunately, not everyone has the simple privilege of understanding their doctor or asking questions in their own language. For some, it requires a family member who's not only fluent in ASL, but also able to take a random Tuesday off work.

We can do better than that, I know it.

While we wait for the systems to improve, know that the simplest thing you can do to help anyone with a communication difference is to *just try*. Say "hi." Write a note on your phone or a piece of paper. Don't ignore someone just because you don't speak their language. A small gesture may not fix the system, but you could make one person's day a little easier, and that's as good a place to start as any.

Key Chapter Takeaways

- Technology has come a long way, but people with communication differences are still often responsible for accommodating themselves.
- In medical settings, family members shouldn't have to be the interpreters. Deaf and HoH patients deserve professional interpreters for medical appointments so their loved ones can simply be present.
- Small efforts can ease high-stress moments, even if it's writing a quick note on your phone to ask if someone needs support.

Prompts for Deeper Reflection

1. Think about your last doctor's appointment. What would it have been like if you couldn't speak directly to your doctor?
2. Do the medical professionals in your life offer interpretation services? What do they look like? Are they reliable?
3. If you saw someone struggling to communicate with staff in a waiting room, would you feel comfortable passing them a note that said "Can I help?" if you knew it'd make a big difference in their day? Why or why not?

CHAPTER 5

THE COST OF SILENCE

y parents had been together for 32 years when my
mom passed away. In a Deaf or HoH household, a
partnership like theirs is about more than love. It's
about survival. They leaned on each other for everything—
communication when no one else understood and
companionship when everyone around them was hearing.

One thing that helped our family heal after losing my mom
was staying connected to the Deaf and HoH community.
That's how my dad met Dixie, and they clicked right away.

To me, it felt like Dad was given a second chance at love, and
I've always believed my mom had something to do with it.
Dixie quickly became like a second mom to me. It was as if
she was meant to be part of our story all along.

Like my mom, Dixie also became Deaf as an infant; it
happened as a reaction to a medication before she was even a
year old. She started going to a school for the Deaf and HoH
when she was six, where she learned ASL and had access to
resources to support her communication needs. But when
she turned 16, Dixie was moved to a mainstream high school

where she no longer had the same accommodations. One year she thrived in a vibrant, language-rich environment; the next, she was isolated in classrooms where no one signed and few people made the effort to connect.

Dixie's experience showed me that even a few good years in the right school can make a lasting difference, but so can the absence of support. Dixie had already developed a strong language foundation by the time she was "mainstreamed," which meant she wasn't as language deprived as some. But that didn't mean she was immune to the impact. It hurts to be left out, no matter how old you are.

Deaf and HoH Culture Insight: "Mainstreaming"

"Mainstreaming" refers to placing Deaf and HoH students into general education classrooms with hearing students, rather than programs designed to meet their communication needs.

Mainstreaming is meant to be inclusive, but it often happens without the right support, like sign language interpreters, note takers, or teachers fluent in ASL.

When I asked my friend Gella, who's Deaf, how early language access shaped her identity, she told me: "I remember that it made me feel like a whole human being to have a language to express myself and be understood, without even needing to use my voice."

Without full access to communication, students may miss out not only on learning opportunities, but also on the connection and sense of belonging that comes with being part of a signing community.

The Impact of Delayed Language Access

My mom, dad, and bonus mom, Dixie, didn't learn to sign until they started school around six years old, which is late considering most kids are exposed to an accessible language from birth. But my friend Stacey's experience was even more extreme.

While my parents went to Deaf boarding schools Monday through Friday from elementary through high school, Stacey didn't grow up with access to Deaf and HoH culture or sign language at all. Instead, she was placed in a mainstream public school and left to figure things out on her own.

Deaf institutions, like the ones my parents attended, often provide more support, but they come with extra costs that some families simply can't afford. Meanwhile, many public schools lack the resources to offer interpreters or ASL instruction, so Deaf and HoH students are expected to get by with lipreading or passing written notes.

Because of this lack of access, Stacey didn't learn ASL until her twenties.

Can you imagine living until adulthood without a language that truly worked for you? Imagine navigating those hard years as a kid, learning how the world works, trying to make friends, dealing with bullies, and feeling self-conscious about your differences, without a way to fully express yourself or understand others.

It's heartbreaking, but unfortunately, Stacey's experience isn't uncommon. Even today, too many Deaf and HoH kids are placed in schools without any interpreters or staff who sign.

How the System Is Supposed to Work

It may surprise the average hearing person that so many Deaf and HoH students still don't get access to the learning environments they need.

My friend Lisa, a Deaf teacher who works at a school for the Deaf and Hard of Hearing, explained that under US law, all children have the right to a Free Appropriate Public Education (FAPE) regardless of their disability. It's up to the schools and districts to meet Deaf and HoH students' needs as part of their Individualized Education Program, but those needs vary more than you might expect.

"Not every Deaf student uses ASL," Lisa explained. Here are a few other ways Deaf and HoH students might communicate and learn best at school:

- **Cochlear implants:** Some Deaf students use spoken language with the help of implants and may not rely on ASL at all.
- **Cued speech:** This is a visual system that uses hand shapes and positions near the mouth to make spoken language easier to lipread.
- **Signing Exact English (SEE):** This sign system follows English grammar and word order more closely than ASL.
- **Pidgin Signed English (PSE):** This is a blend of ASL signs and English word order that's more flexible than SEE. Many Deaf adults don't use "pure" ASL all the time. It's more common to see PSE in daily conversation or classrooms.

- **Note takers:** Trained staff or responsible students type or write real-time summaries or transcripts of what's being said in class.
- **Non-ASL interpreters:** Interpreters may use other modes of communication, like spoken English support, SEE, or another signed language.
- **Oral transliterators:** People silently mouth what's being said so students can lipread more easily, often from a close visual range.

Like Stacey and my parents, many Deaf and HoH students are the only members of their family with any level of hearing loss. In fact, 90–95% of Deaf children have hearing parents who often do not know sign language. As a result, a majority of these children may experience a degree of language deprivation. That means they won't have exposure to an accessible language from birth, which is essential for a child's development.[2]

Parents with Deaf and HoH children often face a steep learning curve. They're tasked with figuring out how best to communicate with their child, often with limited guidance. Even when families are committed to doing the right thing, school systems don't always offer the most supportive accommodations, which makes it harder for these kids to thrive academically and socially.

No Two Children Communicate the Same

My friend Sabrina is hearing, but her son, Cole, has degenerative hearing loss and received a cochlear implant as

---

2   Elizabeth Dougherty, "Getting the Word In," *The Brink*, Boston University, March 6, 2017, https://www.bu.edu/articles/2017/asl-language-acquisition/.

a child. Cole has always chosen to be more verbal and uses little sign language now, but the early exposure he had to ASL set him up with strong communication skills.

Sabrina says the hardest part wasn't learning ASL as a family or adjusting at home. It was navigating the school system. Some districts accommodated Cole's needs well, while others refused to provide an ASL interpreter. Because Cole was verbal, those school districts assumed he didn't need visual language access.

That decision had lasting consequences. As Sabrina put it, "Cole has learned to speak up when he doesn't understand something or hear all of the teacher's instructions, but he still misses out on a lot in his daily classwork."

Sabrina and Cole often have to remind his teachers and friends to repeat themselves and to make sure they're facing him when they speak. It can be frustrating for Cole, but Sabrina says she sometimes feels others growing impatient too.

She wishes more people understood that Cole isn't ignoring them; he just isn't catching everything they're saying. Kids like Cole deserve to participate just as fully as any other student.

The conversation around communication needs goes beyond verbal vs. signed language, and every child's experience has many layers to consider. For example, if a Deaf or HoH student comes to the US from a country where English and ASL aren't primary languages, their language deprivation will likely be more severe.

Imagine a new middle school student whose parents speak Spanish, but her teachers speak English and ASL. She hasn't had access to a signed language until now, so she isn't able to communicate in any of the three languages around her. This scenario is more common than you'd think. These students are forced to navigate a new world without solid communication in any language.

When schools lack the resources to meet the needs of Deaf and HoH students, those children can go years without the right tools to thrive. That may lead to communication struggles, not just at school and not just when they're young, but throughout their lives.

> **Deaf and HoH Culture Insight:**
> **Making Schools More Inclusive**
>
> You don't need to be fluent in ASL to make a difference. Small changes in awareness, access, and design can help create spaces where Deaf and HoH individuals feel welcomed rather than left out.
>
> **Tips for Schools:**
> - Offer ASL as a language credit (or advocate for it).
> - Ensure Deaf and HoH students have access to qualified interpreters.
> - Include Deaf and HoH culture in classroom discussions and diversity programs.
> - Make school events visually accessible. Think captioned videos, a direct view of the person speaking or interpreter, and visual cues like posters or flashing lights.
>
> Even if you're a teacher or parent of hearing children, take time to learn how the school supports Deaf and HoH students and parents. Are there ways you can help advocate for greater access and inclusion? Are there connections you can build to help everyone feel more welcome?

When Kids Don't Have the Words Yet

When Deaf and HoH kids grow up without access to a signed language like ASL, they can experience what's known as language deprivation. This means they miss out on consistent exposure to language during the most critical window of brain development: the first five years.

It can cause more harm than just falling behind in school. Language deprivation can impact emotional development, mental health, self-esteem, and even the ability to form close relationships as children and into adulthood.[3]

Dan, a friend of mine who is Deaf, didn't learn ASL until after high school, not because it wasn't available at school, but because his mom didn't allow it. She believed that if he learned sign language first, he wouldn't have the motivation to speak English. So speech came first.

Dan was placed in a school that only supported oral Deaf students (those who use speech to communicate) and ASL wasn't used or even permitted. He did all of his learning through speech and lipreading. This experience has led Dan to have mixed feelings about the ways he communicates. He told me, "I've felt ambivalent between ASL and English speaking." Today, Dan says he benefits from using both spoken English and ASL, but signing gave him access to a deeper level of emotional expression.

In the Deaf community, there are people who question why he sometimes speaks to communicate instead of signing. But navigating the hearing world as a Deaf person still comes with communication challenges and misunderstandings, even if you choose to speak. I imagine for some that this feels like being caught between two identities.

His story made me wonder how different it must feel for

3 Joseph J. Murray, Wyatte C. Hall, and Kristin Snoddon, "Education and Health of Children with Hearing Loss: The Necessity of Signed Languages," *The Lancet Child & Adolescent Health* 3, no. 10 (2019): 708–709, https://www.ncbi.nlm.nih.gov/pmc/articles/PMC6796673/.

kids to learn, navigate the world, connect with others, and form identities when they aren't absorbing an accessible language from day one. Think about the social cues, tone, and meaning that hearing children naturally absorb from everything around them—conversations they overhear their parents having in the car, people speaking to one another in the grocery store, or the TV that's on as background noise while they play.

Deaf and HoH children don't have that same stream of information unless someone signs it to them. Without adequate access to language, they not only miss out on all that passive learning, they can feel excluded.

I remember going out to eat with Dixie once, and she got upset that my siblings and I spoke English without signing. I guess my parents had gotten used to us doing that, and I didn't realize it would negatively affect her like it did.

But after thinking about how it must've felt for her to navigate high school without anyone around her speaking ASL, I understood her reaction. It must have felt like we were whispering right in front of her and leaving her out of the conversation. No one likes to feel that way.

Dixie helped me see that inclusion looks different for everyone.

It's important to learn what helps each individual feel seen and understood. When families, caregivers, and educators understand how nuanced communication needs can be, they can make decisions that help Deaf and HoH children thrive not just academically, but emotionally and socially too.

Deaf and HoH Culture Insight: Finding Your Voice Without Hearing It

Imagine trying to sing a song you've never heard by relying solely on the vibrations you feel and the movements you observe. For many Deaf and Hard of Hearing individuals, learning to speak involves a similar challenge.

Without the ability to hear their own voice, they often depend on speech therapy to guide them in producing sounds, controlling tone, and modulating volume. This process requires immense dedication, as they have to monitor their speech through tactile feedback and visual cues rather than auditory ones.

Learning to Understand Each Other

Even when school support isn't perfect, the home environment plays a huge role in shaping how Deaf and HoH kids experience the world and their place in it. Parents of Deaf and HoH kids usually fit into one of the following categories:

1. Deaf parents who automatically know how to sign to their child.
2. Hearing parents who feel overwhelmed. They now have to learn a new language and culture on top of raising their child.
3. Hearing parents who already know basic ASL or are educated on how to support their child.

If you're in that second group, I see you. It's a lot to take in. Learning a whole new language while learning to parent is no small feat, especially when you're also juggling work, dishes, bedtime routines, and the occasional meltdown (yours or your kid's!).

But when Lisa told me about her experiences as a Deaf teacher, she reminded me of something I've seen firsthand—access to language isn't about perfection. It's about consistency, effort, and care.

She told me that when a Deaf or HoH child is born to hearing parents who aren't familiar with Deaf culture, there is often a grieving process. Next, some parents may start looking at possible ways to "fix" the hearing loss.

It makes sense. You want your kid to have every advantage in life. But ultimately, access to language is more important than fixing their hearing loss. Lisa told me that by the time a child is seven years old, they have a very difficult time catching up developmentally if they're language deprived.

My parents were lucky enough to learn ASL through their school, but their parents, my grandparents, never signed. They wrote notes to each other and fingerspelled the basics to communicate until my siblings and I were born. After that, we'd interpret for my parents and grandparents during every visit.

We saw that arrangement as normal. But now that I'm a mom, I can't imagine not being able to sit across from my child and just talk to them. I've realized how important it is to reduce communication barriers whenever possible, so you can stay connected in those everyday moments, like asking how their day was or telling them you're proud of them.

Families like mine are scrappy. We find workarounds and, most importantly, we make sure love is always felt. Your willingness to *just try*, even if you stumble, tells your child they're worth it.

Trust me, kids will call you out if you mess up a sign. But they'll also light up when you get it right. That's how understanding begins: one little breakthrough at a time.

The Joys of Early Exposure

I have three grandchildren: Niko, Luna, and Nova. Nova is one year old, and even though my parents are no longer with us, my daughter is teaching her words like "milk" in ASL to pass on our cultural heritage.

Growing up in the Deaf and HoH culture is so much more than just silence and struggle. With the right communication tools, this community offers more connection and joy than I've seen anywhere else. Watching my grandchildren grow has reminded me what it means to be seen and to be understood from the start.

I was holding Nova once at a family gathering while a few adults signed back and forth to each other. I noticed that Nova started moving her hands, trying to mimic what we were doing. It was *so* cute and reminded me of watching my youngest sister, Rose, learn her first signs. Those little hand movements are how it starts.

Now whenever I see Nova, she'll sign to me. Or at least she *thinks* she's signing. This is just like how babies babble when their brains are first starting to make sense of spoken language.

That *"ma-ma-ma-ma-ma"* before they finally say "Mama" still happens for babies whose caregivers communicate using sign language; they just "babble" with their hands instead.

Even if no one in your family communicates using ASL, it's amazing (and fun) to see tiny hands form a sign to tell you what they need for the first time. Try teaching little ones a few signs and watch how proud they are when they sign it back to you for the first time.

Watching Nova learn to express herself in this way has brought back so many memories. It's made me reflect on the gifts and connections I gained by learning ASL and feeling accepted within the Deaf and HoH culture.

How It Gets Better

Stacey didn't access a language that worked for her until adulthood. My grandparents couldn't speak directly with their own children. And kids who don't receive the tools they need to communicate have to work hard to overcome the impact of language deprivation. Things still aren't perfect, but people who care are showing up to help, and it's making a big difference.

Organizations like Language First are doing important work to shift public understanding around language deprivation. They offer clear, evidence-based guidance on helping Deaf and HoH kids access a strong, first language to support their development. If you're a parent or educator looking for resources, visiting their website might be a helpful first step.

I've learned from Deaf and HoH culture that the best remedy for feeling overwhelmed and isolated is a supportive community. So if you're a parent who's new to all of this or just someone looking to show up as an ally, find local connections and reach out. Talk to other families. Ask questions. Listen to stories. Get to know Deaf adults. Find out what helped them learn, thrive, and feel included growing up, and find out what didn't.

Language opens doors and builds vital connections. When we make sure kids have language, we're helping them access what everyone on the planet wants: a sense of belonging.

Key Chapter Takeaways

- Deaf and HoH children need access to a language that works for them, like ASL, during the first five years of life or they can experience language deprivation.
- Language deprivation can impact a child's development, communication, mental health, and self-esteem. Access to language is more important than "fixing" hearing loss.
- You don't have to be fluent in ASL to make a difference in a Deaf or HoH individual's life. Learning a few signs can be a powerful act of connection. Even if you don't know any signs, using gestures can go a long way. Communication doesn't have to be perfect to be meaningful.

Prompts for Deeper Reflection

1. Have you ever made someone feel left out without realizing it? What small change could you make to help others feel included?
2. If someone in your life suddenly lost access to language, how would you support them? Where would you look to find the right tools to communicate?
3. Think about a recent conversation where you felt understood. What led you to feel that way? How can you help someone else feel understood, even if you don't speak the same language?

CHAPTER 6

LOVE'S LEARNING CURVE

Introducing your partner to your dad for the first time can be nerve-racking for anyone, but it can be even more so when they don't speak the same language. When my husband, Chris, was about to meet my dad, I didn't know how it would go. Chris didn't know ASL, and my dad couldn't hear a word he said. As we drove to the campground to spend the weekend with my family, I could tell Chris was getting nervous. But I told him the most important thing: *just try.*

When we pulled up, my dad was already playing horseshoes by the campfire. I brought Chris over and introduced them.

My dad signed, "Have you ever played this before?"

Chris laughed and said, "Hey, I think I played this as a kid. How does it work again?"

Dad raised an eyebrow, grinned, pointed to the stake in the dirt, and signed, "Get it around the pole. Simple. Unless you're bad at it…"

I laughed, handed Chris a horseshoe, and nudged him to throw it at the stake.

The two of them kept their conversation going without me—Chris in spoken English and Dad in ASL—as if there were no language barrier at all. I was nervous about them meeting for no reason!

It was fascinating to watch the two of them get to know each other in their own way without a common language. It reminded me that real connection doesn't always come from perfect communication. Sometimes it's just about staying in the moment and finding common ground. I mean, what father doesn't want to beat his daughter's boyfriend in a backyard game?

Around that time, Chris started taking ASL classes. One of the first things students learn is the alphabet—a sign for each letter—so you can use the alphabet to fingerspell words you don't know. Chris tried that once with my dad.

"G-O-O-D…T-O…S-E-E…Y-O-U…A-G-A-I-N," he spelled out slowly, focusing hard on every letter.

My dad gave him a thumbs up, then signed back with a big smile, "That took forever."

Chris burst out laughing. "Okay, noted. I'll work on my speed."

If you think about it, it'd be challenging for anyone to spell out all of the words you say in a conversation. Chris got points for trying!

Chris showed my dad that he respected him enough to put in the effort, even if it felt unfamiliar. I could simply stand there as a daughter and a girlfriend and watch the two most important men in my life begin to understand each other, without needing to act as the go-between.

After Chris lost a few rounds of horseshoes on that first day, I could already tell Dad liked him, and I liked him even more than before. But the official "welcome to the family" didn't come until later.

Deaf and HoH Culture Insight:
How to Show Up in a Conversation

When hearing people meet someone who's Deaf or HoH, their first instinct is often to talk louder as if the person just needs a volume boost. (Spoiler: They don't!)

I spoke with my friend, Teresa, about ways hearing people can be more supportive when holding a conversation with a member of the Deaf and HoH community. She helped me come up with some great tips:

- **Speak clearly** at a normal volume. Yelling just makes the situation awkward, and nobody wants that.
- **Face the person** so they can see your mouth, facial expressions, and body language.
- **Pause and check in** if they seem confused. Ask if they want you to repeat or clarify.
- **Include them directly in the conversation.** Talk to them, not about them.
- **Write it down** if needed. You can use a piece of paper or your phone. (Find app recommendations in the Resources Section at the back of this book!)

Teresa added, "If you're in a conversation with a Deaf individual and they don't understand you, don't say it doesn't matter or it wasn't important. Try again. It's very frustrating to not understand and feel excluded from the conversation."

Signs of Acceptance

In the Deaf and HoH community, people have "name signs." These are personalized gestures used in sign language instead of fingerspelling people's full names every time. For example, here are the name signs for my siblings and me:

- Mine: The sign for "M" starting at your chin and motioning downward
- Melissa: The sign for "M" at the center of your chest
- Chris: The sign for "C" moving across your forehead
- Ursula: The sign for "U" placed over your heart
- Rose: The sign for "R" tapped on your shoulder
- Ben: The sign for "B-E-N"

(To be honest, I'm not quite sure why we've always spelled out Ben's name while the other siblings got a different name sign. But hey, it stuck!)

Name signs aren't universal. For example, not everyone named Maria has the same name sign as me. That makes name signs incredibly practical. If there's another Maria in the room, having a visual sign makes it easy to clarify which one you're referring to.

You don't choose a name sign for yourself either. They're given to you by a member of the Deaf and HoH community. As CODAs, our parents gave us these names when we were born in addition to the ones on our birth certificates. You could say they're like affectionate nicknames assigned to people in the community. They often include the first letter of your name or a specific personality trait.

Like in any language, friends may have name signs for you that differ from your full name. My friend Nadelle has a funny name sign for me that's different from the one my parents gave me. She gives the "M" some flair, swirling it outward from her head like flowing curls. She says, "It's for my fancy Maria!" It's a nickname she uses because I always have my hair and makeup done. But when she's speaking with others, she'll use my known name sign.

I could change my name sign if I wanted, but keeping it is a way to honor my parents. We typically keep name signs until someone else in the community changes them, and even then we can decide whether to accept the new change.

Name signs should come from a member of the Deaf and HoH community to honor their cultural heritage. Hearing people who aren't born into Deaf or HoH families don't give name signs to others or themselves except in rare cases.

Nadelle became Deaf at two years old and as her hearing parents began learning ASL, they gave her a name sign related to her giggling nature. Later on, her students gave her another nickname that affectionately teased her for moving her mouth when she signs, which isn't customary in Deaf culture. That's not a name she'll keep though. She told me she'll keep the one from her parents unless a Deaf person gives her a more appropriate name.

When Chris started spending more time around my family, my dad mentioned that he needed a name sign too. Chris knew that was an honor; My dad was declaring, "You're one of us." We tossed around a few ideas, but Dad had the final say.

"We'll call him CK," he decided, using the letter "C" followed by a "K" at the temple. That was for Chris Kane, but also a nod to the Calvin Klein logo. My dad always joked that Chris should have been a model, so he thought that double meaning was hilarious.

That's still how I introduce Chris in ASL today: "This is CK."

It's funny how something as simple as a name sign can carry so much weight. Once you've been given one, you're part of the family. For Chris, that meant he was officially part of our world of loud backyard barbecues, clanking tools in the garage, and conversations that bounced between English and ASL.

Welcome to the Family

We joke that the only reason my parents had six kids was because they were Deaf and couldn't hear how loud we were. Add in our partners and children, and our family gatherings turn into joyful chaos complete with dozens of guests, kids shrieking in the sprinkler, and stories told through laughter and hands flying through the air.

One year for Father's Day, we all crowded into the backyard at my dad and bonus mom Dixie's house. Dad grilled meat while my siblings and I chatted, and our kids ran circles around us. At one point, the in-laws (my husband, Chris; Melissa's husband, Matt; Urs's husband, Caine; and my brother Chris's wife, Shay) wandered into the workshop in Dad's garage.

This was where he worked on his favorite projects: building miniature semis from scratch. He ordered parts—rubber wheels, tiny chrome accents, and even working headlights—and assembled them all by hand to sell or give as gifts. The in-laws all loved checking out his latest projects. They'd never seen anything like them before.

They circled one of Dad's newest trucks and commented about how impressive it was. Dad walked up, and they each signed what they could. Matt signed, "C-O-O-L." Shay pointed to the blinking headlights and mouthed, "You made that?"

Without missing a beat, Dad launched into his explanation, signing everything that went into building this truck. They each asked questions and communicated in their own way with a mix of body language, gestures, and the signs they knew.

My dad grabbed a nearly finished truck and motioned for Chris to help with the last step: attaching the second taillight and wiring it to blink in sync with the other one. Chris crouched beside him, took the tools, and followed Dad's instructions.

Everyone else watched as Chris twisted wires, applied a little tape, and with a click, the second taillight blinked on. Dad grinned and signed, "Perfect."

Chris looked up at the other in-laws. "Wait… we just did that without anyone here to interpret for us!"

They all laughed. Over time, they'd each learned our family trait of finding ways to get the job done, even when we need to find quirky workarounds to connect and communicate.

Fun Fact: Want to Talk? Take Off Your Sunglasses.

As a CODA, I'm used to watching people's faces and reading their lips as they speak because those are key aspects of communication in Deaf and HoH culture. Sometimes I don't even realize when the sound is off during a movie until Chris comes in and turns up the volume. When I was growing up, our TV always had closed captions. We didn't need the sound. We just needed to see.

Because visual cues are such an important part of communicating, I can't hold a conversation with someone if they're wearing sunglasses. I need to be able to see how a person's eyes light up and their eyebrows move to fully comprehend what they're saying. Remember that next time you're speaking to a CODA or Deaf or HoH individual. Make sure your eyes and mouth are easy to see!

Social Dynamics Across Languages

I've always seen knowing two languages as a gift. Growing up bilingual made my siblings and me expert multitaskers. We'd carry out full spoken conversations while signing to one another across the room. For example, I can stand in line while my siblings sign their drink orders to me from across a crowded bar. We still do this today.

But speaking ASL in public still draws stares, just like it did when we were kids signing with our parents in the grocery store. Not everyone is used to seeing ASL in everyday spaces. Not everyone knows how to make you feel welcome when you communicate differently. Growing up the way I did means I pick up on that more. I pay attention to who's included, who's left out, and how often access depends on whether others are willing to make space for you.

That awareness became clear at one of my client appreciation parties. We were in the middle of a raffle drawing when a group of Deaf guests started shifting around trying to see. A few hearing people stood directly in front of them, blocking their view of the announcer.

One of my Deaf guests waved from behind them to get the host's attention. He didn't notice her, so she reached into her bag, pulled out a tube of chapstick, and lightly tossed it toward him on the stage.

It hit the stage with a soft thud. That's when I realized what was happening.

"Did she just throw something?" I heard one of the hearing audience members whisper.

I turned and said, "Yeah. She needed to see the host to know what was going on."

I got the host's attention and asked him to direct hearing people to let Deaf and HoH guests move toward the front of the crowd. If they couldn't see the host or an interpreter, they couldn't participate. Period.

Of course, throwing chapstick *isn't* a typical means of getting your point across in the Deaf and HoH culture. But people in this community are accustomed to using visual cues or making adjustments on the fly to communicate.

For example, it's normal to gently move someone aside if

they're blocking a visual conversation. It's the equivalent of saying "excuse me" so the dialogue can continue. Or you might move a centerpiece off the table so you can communicate with the person sitting across from you. These actions aren't seen as rude; it's just how the culture has adapted to life without sound.

I've learned that true connection isn't about perfect communication. It's about showing up, staying open, and making a real effort to meet people where they are. You don't need to speak the same language to create a connection. You simply need to be present, pay attention, and *just try*.

Deaf and HoH Culture Insight: Planning an Event? Here's How to Make It More Inclusive

If you're planning an event with Deaf and HoH guests, remember: Communication is visual. People need to see each other's hands and faces to participate in the conversation.

Here are a few simple ways to make your event more Deaf-friendly:

- Pick a venue with an open floor plan, so it's easy to communicate.
- Avoid standing in front of windows or bright light. The glare can make it hard to see someone's hands or face while they're signing.
- If you have a screen or backdrop, try to use solid colors. Busy patterns can contribute to eye strain.
- Flicker the lights to grab attention instead of clinking glasses.

> - Post a friendly sign: "Please be mindful of where you're standing. Our Deaf and HoH guests need to see each other to communicate!"
>
> Efforts like these help Deaf and HoH participants reduce the fatigue that can come with navigating spaces that aren't designed for them. The event becomes more enjoyable when everyone can participate fully.

Committing to Connection

From spelling out greetings one letter at a time to making tiny taillights blink, the ways we connect with others look different for each of us. Sometimes, love moves through gestures, body language, or simply through helping someone feel seen.

Before my dad passed away, he made a custom truck for each of us—me, my siblings, and our partners, too. Mine is pink and sits in my office where I see it every day. Chris says looking at those trucks always reminds him of that day in the garage, working alongside someone who didn't speak his language and being able to accomplish something together anyway.

Connection doesn't always come easily. It's something you have to commit to despite awkward pauses, misunderstandings, and blunders. But it's worth doing, especially when it's hard. Outlasting the learning curve to build a meaningful connection despite differences can lead to the best rewards and most cherished memories of your life.

Key Chapter Takeaways

- Connection doesn't require perfect communication, just effort. When your communication needs are different from someone else, this can be as simple as following my advice to Chris: *Just try.*
- Small gestures carry big meaning. Whether it's learning a few signs in ASL or working on a project together, real connection usually starts with a simple effort to show you care.
- If you're hosting an event, make sure the space is clear and people can see each other to support Deaf and HoH guests.

Prompts for Deeper Reflection

1. Have you ever been nervous to meet someone new? What would that experience have been like if you didn't speak the same language?
2. Are there any events or communities you're a part of that could be more inclusive to the Deaf and HoH community? How?
3. Is there someone in your life who doesn't quite fit in? What can you do to help them feel more understood?

CHAPTER 7

WHAT IT MEANS TO FEEL UNDERSTOOD

Since my son Rian was born 14 years after my daughter Jordan, he missed out on something I didn't realize would be so hard to recreate: the kitchen table lessons where my mom taught her first grandbaby signs like "milk" and "I love you." They may have felt ordinary back then, but moments like those laid the foundation for our family's commitment to connection and mutual understanding.

Rian has always told me he wished that things had been different. I'd been so wrapped up in raising my kids and growing my business that it was impossible to find the time to make sure we maintained a bilingual home. Without those early experiences of learning sign language while his grandma babysat, Rian couldn't communicate with his grandpa as well as his sister and I could.

So when his high school course catalog landed on our kitchen counter and ASL was listed as a language option, I circled it in red ink. "Pick this one!" This was my chance to finally help Rian learn my first language. It felt like four gifts in one: a way to strengthen Rian's relationship with his grandfather, keep my mom's legacy alive, make up for not teaching him ASL sooner, and help him get an easy A in the class. A total win all around.

"This will be awesome," I said with a wink. "I can help with your homework!"

Spoiler alert: It was a disaster.

It turns out that there's a huge difference between being taught ASL in a classroom and learning it as your first language. Rian would come home and show me signs I wasn't used to seeing—some I'd learned a completely different way.

One night, he signed "birthday" exactly how his teacher had taught him: touching his middle finger to his chin and then his chest.

I smiled and said, "Here's how I sign it."

With both palms up, I placed one hand over the other to sign the word "birth." Then, I held one arm flat in front of me and let the other sweep down like the sun setting, to sign the word "day." I'd learned it that way growing up on the East Coast, and I thought it was cool that I could teach my kid authentic sayings he wasn't learning in school.

The next day, Rian tried to impress his teacher with the new sign he'd learned from me, but she told him to stick with the vocabulary she'd taught him. Turns out, I wasn't the rockstar ASL tutor I thought I would be.

Eventually, Rian realized my native way of communicating in ASL wasn't what he was learning at school. But I insisted on helping him with a test in a last-ditch attempt to use my ASL skills to his advantage.

He looked skeptical. "Are you *sure* you can help me?"

"We've got this in the bag," I said confidently.

So I helped him through the take-home test, thinking to myself, "How great is this? Who else has a CODA parent who can help them ace the ASL test?" I was finally teaching my son my first language and felt like such a "cool mom."

That is, until the following week when Rian walked in after school. He dropped his graded test on the kitchen counter and gave me a look.

We'd flunked it.

Rian has always been a straight-A student, so getting anything lower than an A was a big deal for him.

"Mom, thanks a lot!"

I shrugged. "You're welcome. Anytime you need help failing an ASL test, you know who to call."

We laugh about it now, but it did make me think. For the first time, I saw how different it was to learn this language versus living it.

Even though I didn't win any awards for my ASL tutoring skills, I remember the first time Rian could communicate on a Sunday FaceTime session with his grandpa without my help. I watched them go back and forth, my dad grinning ear to ear while making fun of my cooking skills and Rian laughing when he understood.

Rian closed the laptop and said, "I get why you love this so much." At that moment, no one cared about grammar or getting the answer right. The only thing that mattered was a grandfather and grandson enjoying each other's company. That sense of connection is something we all deserve.

Fun Fact: Sign Language Is Different Everywhere

Did you know that ASL is one of more than 300 signed languages worldwide?

ASL is the most commonly used signed language in the US, but signs can vary from state to state. Growing up on the East Coast, I learned different signs for the words "favorite" and "birthday" than what people use in Colorado, where I live now. I like to think of these variations as equivalent to "accents" in ASL.

Here are a few other interesting signed languages to show you how varied they can be.

ISN (Idioma de Señas de Nicaragua, or Nicaraguan Sign Language): ISN was created by Deaf children in the 1980s spontaneously and without influence from other signed languages. Before that point, Nicaragua didn't have an official signed language, but now Deaf and HoH Nicaraguans can communicate fluently in ISN.

BSL (British Sign Language): BSL is completely different from ASL, even though England and the US share the common language of English. For example, BSL uses a two-handed fingerspelling alphabet while ASL uses one hand to sign letters. ASL is actually more closely related to French Sign Language than British Sign Language.

Learned Language vs. Lived Language

I have a lot of respect for interpreters and family members who learn ASL when it's not their native language, because it's a completely different way of communicating. This is a culture with facial expressions, eye contact, inside jokes, and ways of thinking that don't always fit neatly into an academic box.

I'm not the only one who's experienced the gap between textbook signs and real-life expressions. One mom, Amber, told me about a moment that perfectly captured this difference between learning and living the language and the funny misunderstandings that can happen along the way.

Amber's daughter, who is Deaf, was trying to ask a question about the menstrual cycle, but she accidentally signed "period," which more like the sign for "dentist."

Amber told me, "I gave her a confused look, and then she signed 'vagina dentist' which made me even more confused. I laughed and told her that vaginas don't have teeth. Then she signed 'vagina bleeding' and I finally figured out what the heck she actually meant!"

The mix-ups that come from learning sign language to communicate with a family member can be frustrating, but other times they can be pretty hilarious. Amber's experience helped me see why I wasn't able to help Rian like I thought could.

People don't usually communicate exactly like the textbook version of a language. We make the language work for us.

Plus, I never learned "textbook ASL." I was using the native version of a language passed down in my family, shaped by community, emotion, and a lifetime of living in the language.

That said, the gifts of living between two languages and two cultures do show up in unexpected places for me now, like real estate closings.

Around 80% of my clients are Deaf and HoH, and I always bring interpreters to our closings. After everything we went through with my parents' medical appointments, I know how critical it is to have someone there whose only job is to make sure everyone understands each other. It allows me to focus on my work as a real estate agent while knowing communication isn't falling through the cracks. But even with professionals in the room, I find myself jumping in out of instinct.

Not long ago, I attended a real estate closing with Liz, an interpreter I work with often. She's skilled, experienced, and I trust her completely. However, as the lender started explaining some of the financial disclosures, I could see my client's expression shift. Something wasn't landing.

So right in the middle of Liz's interpreting, I jumped in and started signing to make sure the client understood everything. As I've mentioned, I'm not a professional interpreter and my way of signing may not be as polished, but it does help in some situations like this. The lightbulb clicked for my client, and just like that, we were all back on the same page.

Afterward, I turned to Liz and said, "Sorry! Sometimes I forget that this is *your* job, not mine."

She laughed. "You can't help it. You were raised to do this!"

It's true. Sometimes the nuances in my non-academic version of ASL can support understanding if a conversation gets stuck. It's like the difference between learning Italian from a textbook and learning it from your nonna while she's stirring a pot of Sunday sauce. The textbook learner may have a better understanding of grammar rules. On the other hand, the one who grew up living in the language could be better equipped to have a conversation with a native speaker using Italian slang and gestures.

I have deep gratitude for the ASL interpreters who've supported my family and me over the years. My mom always thought interpreting would be the perfect job for me. I was fluent in ASL, I was good with people, and I'd been interpreting informally my whole life. But I never really wanted to, partly because I can't speak English and sign at the same time to save my life! My experience within the Deaf and HofH community has taught me to appreciate others for the unique gifts they offer the world.

> **Deaf and HoH Culture Insight: Interpreter Spotlight**
>
> Concert interpreters have gotten well-deserved recognition in recent years for their expressive stage presence. Several have gone viral for delivering passionate performances so the Deaf and HoH crowd can experience the full energy of the music.
>
> One band known for consistently showing up for their Deaf and HoH fans is the Grateful Dead. While their hearing fans are affectionately called "Deadheads," the band has also cultivated a devoted community of "Deafheads."
>
> Sometimes an interpretation can look impressive but be hard to understand for a signing audience. That's not the case with the Grateful Dead. They're known for having interpreters who convey the literal meaning of each song, so Deaf fans can follow the lyrics and emotional arc of a song in real time.

The Goal? Joyful Inclusion

When Rian came out as gay at 12 years old, it wasn't a big, dramatic family moment. It was just…love. My siblings showed up in the same way. They met Rian with total acceptance and didn't skip a beat. Of course, I already knew (mothers often do), and the second he told me, my response was simple:

"Okay. I love you. What do you need?"

There was no panic around figuring out how to be a supportive parent. I already knew how to do that. I learned how from my parents and the community I grew up in. Growing up in the Deaf and HoH community taught me to have empathy for people who have different life experiences than my own. This community is incredibly compassionate. They naturally include other marginalized groups in their events and conversations, maybe because they've felt caught on the "outside" often, and they want to help others who feel that way, too.

When you grow up around people who are misunderstood, you learn to read between the lines. You pick up on moments when people don't feel safe to speak their truth. You look out for what they need to feel welcome, especially when they're surrounded by people who don't share their experiences.

I may not have done a perfect job passing down ASL to my children, but there's one lesson I was determined to teach them: Everyone deserves to feel seen and supported for who they are.

My kids grew up hearing that you never know what someone else is carrying. They could be Deaf or HoH. Maybe they're neurodivergent. Perhaps they're grieving or overcoming a traumatic experience. Or maybe they're the only member of the LGBTQ+ community in the room. I wanted to raise my kids to be the kind of people who notice and make space for others.

That's the message I hope to convey from the Deaf and HoH community. Compassion and empathy are often the greatest gifts you can give the people you love, especially when they come to you with something you don't quite understand.

If you were born blind, wouldn't you hope an adult would buy you a cane to navigate the world safely and independently?

If you were born Deaf, wouldn't you want the ability to communicate directly with the people you love?

If you had a vulnerable truth about your identity that you were afraid to share, wouldn't you want to be met with a hug?

You don't have to do any of this perfectly. Especially with parenting, there's no way to avoid mistakes. The important thing is that you show up anyway.

My son-in-law, Andrew, once shared something with me that I've never forgotten. After visiting our house early in his relationship with my daughter he told me: "There were moments when the room went completely silent. At first, I was confused. But when I scanned the room, I noticed you all were still having conversations, just in ASL."

Andrew had never experienced a situation like that before because he didn't grow up around anyone who was Deaf or spoke using sign language.

He continued, "It was kind of beautiful in a way. All I'd ever known was speaking out loud. That night made me want to take an ASL class with Jordan so she could relearn and I could learn enough to communicate better with Ray."

That's what it's all about when things are different from your norm—leaning in rather than turning away, getting curious, trying to connect, and finding the beauty in another person's way of doing things.

There are opportunities to meet others with this kind of love and support every day. When you start embracing them, you see just how much your small efforts can change someone's life for the better.

How Love Spreads

Because our family openly embraces Rian's identity, I have parents reach out to ask me how they can support their child who has come out as a member of the LGBTQ+ community.

A few years ago, a friend shared that her daughter, let's call her Ashley, had come out as transgender. Ashley was born Deaf and had always struggled to express who she was. When she finally found the courage to tell her parents "I'm a girl" at 16 years old, her father tried to send her to a conversion therapy camp. He decided she was possessed by the devil and cut off contact with her.

But Ashley's mom knew her daughter. She knew Ashley wouldn't subject herself to family rejection, social isolation, and potential violence unless the pain she felt *hiding* this part of herself was more painful than those risks. She believed her daughter and wanted to support her through this, but she wasn't sure how.

I told her the same thing I told my family when Rian came out as gay: "You don't have to get it perfect. Just show up. *Just try.*"

That's what she did. She helped Ashley change her name and gender marker legally. She bought her new clothes and signed up for family therapy. And most importantly, she didn't let Ashley's father make her feel ashamed of her child.

Another thing I told Ashley's mom was to lean into the Deaf community. "They've got you," I said without a shadow of a doubt.

Ashley was raised in Deaf schools. Most of her friends and teachers already knew what it meant to live in a world not built for you. They rallied around Ashley and her mom right away, and they even gave her a new name sign.

It wasn't even a question of whether she'd be accepted. It was: "How can we show up for you?"

When I hear people ask what inclusive really means, I think of stories like Ashley's. I think about how much the Deaf and HoH culture has taught me about what it means to be not only accepted, but cherished, for who you are.

Fun Fact: Meet These Deaf Drag Queens

If you've never seen Deafies in Drag, do yourself a favor and look up their videos. Selena Minogue and Casavina are a hilarious duo I'm lucky enough to know personally. They create educational content and viral videos that blend Deaf culture, comedy, and drag.

Their performances are a delightful intersection of Deaf and LGBTQ+ identities. Hearing people will learn new things about these communities from their videos, and Deaf and HoH folks might watch and think, "Wow, they get it!"

Celebrating One Another

The more we learn to lean into each other's worlds instead of turning away, the richer all of our lives become. That's what community does best. It shows us how to love each other better, and the whole world is better for it.

Shortly after Rian came out, I attended a DOVE (Deaf Overcoming Violence through Empowerment) event wearing a rainbow pin. It was the first time I'd done something like that, so I had a heightened awareness of how people might react going into the event.

As soon as I opened the door, I saw volunteers wearing DOVE t-shirts. I hadn't realized before, but the organization's shirts had the rainbow flag incorporated into the design! I don't know why I was surprised. Inclusion is so ingrained in the Deaf and HoH culture. I realized these weren't separate conversations. Deaf, queer, survivor, advocate…all of these identities belonged in the same space.

As humans, we're wired to fear what we don't understand. But you know what else is wired into us? The need for belonging. We need each other. We thrive in community, especially when we feel seen and celebrated.

I've learned from watching Deaf *and* LGBTQ+ families that people flourish when they're accepted. When hearing families embrace a Deaf child, that child is more likely to thrive because they're given access to language, support, and pride in who they are. When straight parents embrace a queer or trans child, that child has a better shot at thriving too.

To me, that's what love is: Letting people show up as the fullest, richest version of themselves (even if their authentic self differs from your expectations) and saying, "You're safe here. I've got you." It doesn't have to be complicated. A hug, a shared laugh, or a simple "you're loved" can make a huge difference to someone who's used to feeling like an outsider.

When people can access a sense of true community and belonging, they can finally feel safe, honored, and affirmed for their authentic selves. They don't lose their sparkle. They get to keep it and let it shine.

Instead of surviving or getting by, they get to *live*. Everyone deserves that.

Key Chapter Takeaways

- Living a language is different from learning it. Whenever you can, immerse yourself in the *culture* rather than just learning from a textbook.
- Connection doesn't require perfect grammar. You don't need to be an expert to make someone feel seen and understood. Presence and effort go a long way.
- When people are embraced for who they are, they thrive. The Deaf, HoH, and LGBTQ+ communities remind us that access and acceptance change lives.

Prompts for Deeper Reflection

1. Think of a time when someone tried to connect with you in a language, skill, or culture that wasn't their own. How did their effort make you feel?
2. Have you ever hesitated to support someone because you didn't know the "right" thing to say? What might it look like to show up imperfectly?
3. What communities or identities do you feel less familiar with? How might learning more, through stories, friendships, or even showing up to a community event, enrich your world?

Part 3

A MORE INCLUSIVE WORLD

CHAPTER 8

WORKPLACE REALITIES

L ong before I built a career serving Deaf and HoH homebuyers and sellers, I found myself sitting in the lobby of a mortgage company, waiting to interview for my first job. I was just 16, the youngest candidate in the room by far. But I already had a child to raise and rent to pay, and I was determined to compensate my mom for babysitting.

As I waited for my interview, I shuffled some papers in my lap and tried to keep myself focused. I had a salary number I kept repeating in my head: $24,000. I'd practiced it so many times, I still remember it today.

I didn't know what a normal salary was, but I'd run the numbers as well as any brand-new teenage mom could. At the time, that felt like enough to take care of Jordan and keep a roof over our heads. Supporting her was my primary motivator. I wasn't just interviewing for pocket money like other kids my age. I was sitting in that chair, sweating through my clothes, because I had my own family to provide for now.

My childhood as a CODA taught me that you have to push forward and figure things out, even when you're scared and winging it. This was just another day where I had to hold my own in a room full of adults. I was nervous, but in a way, I'd been training my whole life for this.

"Maria?" A woman called me back to the interview room.

We both sat down, and she started asking questions. She seemed surprised at how familiar I was with the finance and mortgage terms she brought up. I explained that I'd helped my parents buy a house when I was 12—atypical work experience, but it seemed to win me some points.

As the interview came to a close, she asked the question I'd anticipated most:

"What are your salary expectations?"

I had the number burned into my mind, but all I managed to get out at that moment was "24."

There was a pause, just long enough for me to panic, and then a polite nod. The interviewer thanked me, and I left, worried that I'd blown it.

But a week later, the offer came in the mail. The contract read: $2,400 per month. I stared at the number, did the math in my head, and looked at it again just to be sure. I had said "24," meaning $24,000 *per year*. They thought I meant $2,400 *per month*.

The company was offering $400 more per month than I'd imagined possible! I may have stumbled over my words, but my "fake-it-till-you-make-it" CODA confidence had worked in my favor. I hadn't just landed the job. I'd scored us more diaper money and a little extra breathing room as I tried to figure out this whole motherhood thing.

Moments like that always point me back to something my childhood taught me: how much access matters. I had stumbled and guessed my way through a professional interaction and ended up faring better than I even imagined. My Deaf and HoH friends and family often have to go above and beyond just to prove they belong, without the tools they need to communicate.

What if it were my dad in that interview chair doing his best to provide for me as a baby? Would he have been jumping up and down with an offer letter in hand like I was? There were no accommodations available during that interview—I was never asked if I needed any. And there certainly wasn't an ASL interpreter available.

Learn ASL: "Do You Need an Interpreter?"

If someone lets you know that they're Deaf or HoH, you can ask if they need an interpreter to create a more welcoming environment from the start. Here's a simple way to sign this question in ASL.

1. **You**: Point forward, toward the person you're addressing.
2. **Need**: Sign the letter "X" (hold your index finger up and curve it like a hook), then bend it downward sharply once.
3. **Interpreter**: Sign the letter "F" with both hands (thumb and index finger forming a circle, like the "ok" sign). Touch the circles together where your thumbs and index fingers meet, and then twist one hand forward.

---

4. **Eyebrows up**: In ASL grammar, yes/no questions are shown with raised eyebrows and a slight head tilt forward.

If the person makes a fist and bobs it up and down, that means "yes." It's okay if you don't have an interpreter around you. You can use a free VRS app like **Sorenson VRS** to connect with a certified ASL interpreter in real time. Just remember to ask before calling on someone's behalf.

What Are Workplace Accommodations?

If you don't know many people with a disability or communication needs different from yours, you may not be familiar with workplace accommodations. That's okay. Most of us aren't taught about these things unless they affect us directly.

If this is a new concept, workplace accommodations are adjustments or supports that allow someone with a disability to do their job effectively and safely. That might mean offering an ASL interpreter for meetings, providing captions on training videos, or sharing important information in writing instead of only saying it out loud in a crowded room.

Workplace accommodations aren't just something you should offer as an act of kindness. They're legal rights under the Americans with Disabilities Act (ADA), which includes protections for Deaf and HoH workers like:

- Reasonable accommodations must be provided to help an employee do their job. This can include the use of interpreters, visual alerts, or flexible communication methods.

- It's illegal to discriminate against qualified workers based on a disability.
- Employers can't deny someone an opportunity because of assumptions about what they can and can't do.

Although reasonable workplace accommodations are required by law, that doesn't mean they're always offered without the person having to advocate hard for themselves first. My dad worked dozens of different jobs over the years and never had an interpreter in the room for a work meeting. Not once.

Dad handled these things with humor most of the time. He used to say he didn't belong in the typical workforce anyway. His dream job was to be in the Mafia—the tough guy watching everyone's back. He always called himself "the Godfather." But he'd laugh and add, "I couldn't hear anyone sneaking up behind me...so I wouldn't last a day!"

Communication Tip: Check Your Assumptions

I like to believe most of us are good people who want to be kind and supportive. But we don't always realize the subconscious biases we've picked up from living in a world that wasn't built with everyone in mind. Sometimes, these beliefs show up in the workplace without anyone meaning harm.

- **Audism** is the belief that hearing people are superior to Deaf or HoH people.

- **Ableism** is the assumption that people are more valuable or capable if they move, think, or communicate in "typical" ways. This can affect how we view and treat people with visible disabilities (like someone using a wheelchair) *and* invisible ones (like an autistic person with sensory processing differences).

You might think, "Of course I don't feel that way." But these biases often show up unconsciously, like assuming someone isn't a fit for a client-facing role or speaking to an interpreter instead of the Deaf person in the room.

My friend Angie, who is hearing but works with the Deaf and HoH community at a nonprofit, told me that she's seen how hearing people can come across as talking down to those with hearing loss, even if it's unintentional. She says, "Hearing loss has nothing to do with intelligence. People should try to understand differences instead of judging what they don't know."

This isn't about guilt, and I'm not here to speak for everyone. But a little awareness goes a long way. No matter who you are, it's worth getting curious about your relationship with these concepts, so you can treat others (and yourself!) with more respect and compassion.

How Deaf and HoH Workers Get Left Out

Our parents' careers influence most of us to some degree. We might follow in their footsteps, go into the family business, or make an intentional choice to take a different path. In my case, my parents' work stories made me want to make the world better for the people I'd seen get left out during my childhood.

My dad was a mechanic by trade and started out fixing helicopters, but he was always drawn to fast cars. His favorite part was the roar of the engine. He didn't need to hear it to love that deep rush of power you feel in your chest.

Some of my favorite family memories are of us going to Bandimere Speedway to watch the "funny cars" race while the bleachers shook beneath us. My dad loved feeling their power vibrate everything around us as they flew past. He knew everything there was to know about those cars, and he loved sharing that world with us. But outside our family bubble, the world didn't celebrate his passion the same way.

Across his whole career, my dad never once got a raise or a promotion. He was afraid to ask because he knew it'd be hard to find another job as a Deaf mechanic if they let him go. Dad once held down five jobs just to support our family: his mechanic gig, two newspaper deliveries, shifts at the auto parts store, and he even tagged along with me to sell water softeners door-to-door when I did a stint working for an MLM.

Dad always showed up early, stayed late, and went above and beyond for his team. He had the skills, the dedication, and the drive to go further, but without access to communication, those qualities were often invisible to the people in charge.

My mom had a similar experience. She was a stay-at-home mom for most of our childhood, but there came a time when she applied to work at a fast food restaurant to help make ends meet. During the interview, she had to write back and forth on a notepad to communicate. She got the job, but they stuck her in the back because they assumed she couldn't take orders, and they never stopped to ask what she *could* do.

That's the reality when workplaces are built on the assumption that everyone hears. Deaf and HoH people are more likely to be left out of conversations, promotions, and community. It's not that they can't do the job. They can do everything other than hear. But jobs aren't often built for them to leverage the unique skills they bring to the table.

Deaf and HoH Culture Insight: "Deaf Gain"

A common assumption is that hearing loss is a negative thing—you lack something you *should* have. The concept of "Deaf Gain" flips that script.

Instead of focusing on what's missing, Deaf Gain emphasizes what's *gained* through being Deaf or HoH, like access to a vibrant culture with its own language, deep community bonds, and unique strengths. For example, people in the Deaf and HoH community may develop exceptional skills in spatial awareness, attention to detail, creative problem solving, or nonverbal communication.

Acceptance shouldn't mean helping people assimilate to the norm. Instead, we should recognize and value the strengths everyone has, even when they don't match traditional expectations. Looking at differences this way can help us build more inclusive workplaces *and* benefit more from untapped talents in the workforce.

From Awareness to Workplace Advocacy

Growing up in the Deaf and HoH community, I gained countless skills that I use in my work. I'm one of a very small handful of real estate agents in Colorado who are fluent in ASL. I use those language skills daily, but there are more subtle tools I carry with me too. Since ASL doesn't rely on tone of voice to convey emotions like joy, frustration, urgency, or reassurance, I know I need to communicate these things with facial expressions, body language, or even emojis.

My colleague, Vicki, told me it took her a while to learn those nuances in communication. She's a mortgage lender who's hearing, but she has served Deaf and HoH clients for more than a decade. The first few years, she relied heavily on the technical aspects of communication.

Vicki said, "I focused on clear emails, straightforward instructions, and the occasional interpreted phone call. But something was missing."

She decided to be more intentional about expressing emotion, especially during traction points in the loan process. She started wording her emails to come across more empathetic and human. She used more video messages with facial expressions, and tried to maintain a more compassionate tone on interpreted calls.

Vicki realized that even with interpreters present, it's important to remember that the mortgage process comes with financial jargon and emotional ups and downs. It can be a frustrating experience for anyone. But without hearing the compassion in her voice, her Deaf and HoH clients needed a unique approach to feel as seen and supported as she wanted them to be.

Sometimes, inclusion is as simple as being more intentional with your communication. Other times, it means pushing back when the system gets it wrong.

I once saw a client almost get wrongfully charged for an interpreter fee. It showed up on the closing statement like it was just another service. But under the ADA, buyers and sellers can't be charged for accommodations related to their disability. That isn't the client's responsibility. I had it removed before the client saw it, but only because I knew their rights.

Another time, I had Deaf clients come to me after attending homebuyer education classes put on by CHFA (Colorado Housing and Finance Authority). These classes help people understand important aspects of the process, like how to qualify for a mortgage. But there were no interpreters, closed captions, or any real ways for them to access the information the rest of the class was learning.

I called CHFA, the state, and whoever else would pick up the phone. I asked key decision-makers why accessibility wasn't already built into these classes. I explained that these weren't extra services. They were required accommodations under the ADA.

Eventually, they listened. Now, CHFA provides interpreters for in-person classes and closed captioning for online sessions. It's something that doesn't affect most hearing participants at all but for the Deaf and HoH community, it means they can benefit from these programs for the first time. Lack of access like this often isn't intentional; many of us simply don't stop to consider how inaccessible the world is for people whose needs differ from our own.

But once you start noticing, you can't unsee it. You can ask better questions, speak up in meetings, or make small changes that open the door a little wider for someone else.

Communication Tip: A Note on Language

"Deaf" and "disabled" are not bad words. They're not insults. They're identities. That said, language is personal. The best approach is to ask people how they'd like to be referred to and then listen.

It's worth paying attention to the common sayings many of us pick up because some are more harmful than we might realize. People often say, "I'm not Deaf" when they mean "I heard you." When I hear that, I respond, "No, but my parents are." It's not meant to shame, just to invite a moment of reflection.

Here are some everyday phrases to rethink and more inclusive swaps to try:

- Instead of "falling on deaf ears," try "it was ignored."
- Instead of "the blind leading the blind," try "they don't know what they're doing."
- Instead of "Are you deaf?" try "Did you catch that?"
- Instead of "turn a blind eye," try "ignore the problem."
- Instead of "that's dumb," try "that doesn't work for me."
- Instead of "that was tone-deaf," try "that was insensitive."

In workplaces and public spaces that aim to welcome *everyone*—words matter. Reframing your language makes space for more people to feel safe and included, without needing to explain why a phrase stings.

My Own Deaf Gain

Yes, on the whole, accessibility isn't where it should be. Hearing people still carry more privileges in most professional settings than the Deaf and HoH community. Even so, the last thing I want is for anyone to feel sorry for my parents or for the community I grew up in. What I hope you see instead are examples of strength and the kind of resilience that shouldn't be required—but often is.

The Deaf and HoH community has a different way of moving through the world—one that's rooted in presence and attunement to the needs of others. If more workplaces embraced those values, we'd all be better for it.

I've never been made to feel more like I belong than when I'm in a room surrounded by the Deaf and HoH community. People look out for each other. They pull you into the conversation so you're not left out. I hope to spread that feeling to anyone who's felt like an outsider in work or life.

Where You Come In

You don't have to be immersed in the Deaf and HoH community to make a difference. Here are a few small actions anyone can take:

- **Ask before assuming:** My friend Cindy recommends not assuming that a Deaf or HoH person can understand a summary of a conversation or fast speech even if they can speak. Be sure to ask what they need and make sure they're catching everything.

- **Budget for access:** Build interpreter services, captions, and written materials into your event plans, onboarding, and meetings from the start.

- **Don't talk *to* the interpreter:** If you're speaking to a Deaf or HoH conversation partner, address them directly. The interpreter is there to facilitate, not speak for anyone.

- **Caption your videos and training:** Automatically generated captions are better than nothing, but they often get it wrong. Outsourcing real captions is easy to do and makes your content more accessible to *everyone*. Too often, Deaf creators end up doing the extra work of adding captions themselves so others can understand their message. Let's share that responsibility from the start.

- **Normalize visual cues:** In group settings, flick the lights on and off to get attention. Don't block your mouth when talking. If you're wearing a mask, consider a clear one.

- **Notice how people are left out:** Is a coworker missing the punchline that everyone is laughing at? Is important information being shared only verbally? Inclusion starts with paying attention.

Making your workplace or business more supportive of the Deaf and HoH community is worthwhile, and the ripple effects can stretch far beyond your office. When we build spaces that work for this community, we create a world that works better for everyone.

Key Chapter Takeaways

- Providing reasonable accommodations for people with different communication needs is a legal requirement through the ADA.
- Deaf and HoH workers are often left out, not because they can't do the job, but because the workplace often isn't built to leverage their strengths.
- Deaf Gain is a term that reflects the vibrant relationships, language, culture, skills, and gifts one gains from belonging to the Deaf and HoH community.

Prompts for Deeper Reflection

1. Have you ever been in a situation where you didn't understand something important and were expected to just "go along with it?" How did that make you feel? What would have helped?
2. What assumptions do you make about how people should communicate at work?
3. Could you provide more communication options in your workplace, like putting meeting summaries in writing or making sure your team knows how to use VRS apps if needed?

CHAPTER 9

ADULTING IN THE HEARING WORLD

You've seen me come back to the phrase *just try* again and again. To me, these are words to live by when connecting with anyone whose communication needs differ from yours. The best connections in life start when someone leans in instead of backing away. One of my favorite examples of that came from my friend Lori.

She was the only Deaf student at her small-town high school and wore hearing aids from the age of two. She went to a local teen dance during one summer break—picture lights flashing around a gymnasium, the smells of perfume and popcorn in the air, and music vibrating the floor. Lori stood near the edge of the crowd and felt the bass in her chest as kids around her moved to the beat. A boy from another town spotted her and walked over. He leaned in close to say something in her ear over the noise. She didn't react at first.

"He pulled back and looked at me, as if he was waiting for an answer," Lori told me. "I couldn't tell what he asked, so I let him know that I was Deaf. Then, I showed him how to look at my face and speak slowly so I could read his lips. I could tell he was shocked and a little nervous at first. Then he asked if I could even enjoy the music."

She told him the truth. She'd been dancing since she was little with her dad, and while she couldn't understand the lyrics, she could still feel the beat. Lori and the boy danced and enjoyed the evening together, and he asked if he could see her again. The two of them dated for a while before heading off to college.

"After we connected over music, he even wrote me a song," Lori shared.

That boy could have let his nerves get the best of him. He could've missed out on a meaningful chance to connect with Lori. Instead, he chose to pause, ask questions, and explore the connection rather than stepping away. He decided to *just try.*

Entering adulthood is hard enough without communication barriers impacting important experiences like dating. We each have the power to make it slightly easier for one another by leading with kindness. That mindset can turn an awkward moment into a beautiful memory.

But what about the other significant moments we navigate as adults? Buying a home, having a baby, getting married, and other big events present unique challenges and opportunities for connection for the Deaf and HoH community, too. That's what this chapter is about. Unless you've lived it, you might not realize how much communication access shapes everything from understanding your child's vows on their wedding day to advocating for yourself while giving birth.

Understanding Life's Big Moments

As an adult, much of life is spent either celebrating important moments or filling out paperwork for those moments: marriage licenses, funeral programs, birth certificates, or closing paperwork for your first home. But for those in the Deaf and HoH community, major life events come with an extra to-do list item: interpretation logistics.

Who will interpret? Will they understand our signing style? Will we all be able to follow along in real time, or will we miss something important?

We had Father Tom, our family's longtime priest, at my sister Melissa's wedding. Father Tom already knew ASL, and he officiated the wedding and signed the entire ceremony himself.

During the vows, I glanced over at my dad. His eyes, locked on Father Tom's hands, glistened with pride. He didn't need me to whisper what was happening or nudge him to stand at the right time. He could be fully present, and so could my siblings and I. We didn't have to make sure everyone knew what was going on. Instead, I could just be the sister of the bride, soaking in the moment alongside everyone else.

Because Father Tom made the effort to learn ASL, he can lead weddings and funerals in a way that includes Deaf and HoH family members. Funerals are already hard enough on the family; the priest knowing ASL saves them from the extra step and expense of hiring an interpreter. It means they can honor their loved ones and be part of the service without straining to catch the meaning behind someone else's words.

Not every celebration goes that smoothly, but I've learned that access can show up in unexpected ways. Even people who don't know sign language at all can make a difference by showing a willingness to *just try*.

Communication Tip: Accessible Weddings

In chapter 6, we discussed the importance of making events more inclusive, especially when Deaf or HoH loved ones are part of the celebration. Weddings are no exception. Here are a few ways to make sure everyone feels fully included on your big day:

- **Hire a qualified interpreter** who is comfortable with the pace and tone of ceremonies. Book them early and meet ahead of time so they can get familiar with specifics like the couple's signing style or any religious or cultural terms.
- **Consider visibility when planning your layout.** Can your Deaf guests clearly see the interpreter or officiant? Are they seated close enough to the action?
- **Include ASL in the ceremony or vows.** Even learning to sign a short phrase like "I love you" or "thank you for being here" can make a huge impact.
- **Use captions on videos or slideshows**, and provide scripts or programs with important moments written out so everyone can follow along.

> • **Check with your guests.** Don't be afraid to ask what would help them feel most comfortable. Access isn't one size fits all.
>
> Love, communication, accessibility, and inclusion are deliberate choices we make every day. They each have the power to support connection and improve all of our lives for the better.

Deaf-Friendly Homes

Everything, from big life moments to the spaces we live in, is easier when communication feels natural. When I was a kid, I didn't know the phrase "Deaf-friendly." We just called it home. It turns out my childhood home *was* an example of Deaf-friendly design. It was the kind of space I now help real estate clients find when they're ready to buy.

Deaf-friendly home design means an open floor plan. In my house growing up, if my mom was folding laundry and needed to ask which of us left our muddy shoes on the floor, she could sign it across the room and we'd all see. Hearing families can yell across the house to get each other's attention, but that's not how it works for families like mine. Having clear views between common spaces meant we could communicate without having to chase each other around the house. (Although, my siblings and I still did that often!)

One of my first Deaf clients was Danielle, a single mom buying her first house. I could feel it the moment we stepped into the unit: open kitchen, clear views to the dining area, big windows that filled the space with light. I saw her eyes move from wall to wall, calculating like I was.

"You'll love this," I signed. "You can see the front door *and* the oven from the couch."

Danielle grinned. She'd been working with another real estate agent before we met, and she was relieved that I understood her lifestyle without needing an explanation.

To this day, I can't stand a kitchen that's closed off to the rest of the house. That's the room where all of the best things happen—family recipes are shared, birthday cakes are decorated, and late-night snacks are thrown together. Separating the kitchen from the rest of the home means you miss out on connection, whether or not you have Deaf or HoH family members.

Danielle and her son ended up moving into that house, and I realized how passionate I was about helping the Deaf and HoH community navigate the real estate process. It's an honor to play a role in making what can be a daunting experience more accessible and welcoming. Over the years, it's become second nature to me. But my colleague Dan once told me that watching my Deaf and HoH clients walk into the closing room shifted how he thought about the process of buying or selling a home.

"It's hard enough to understand real estate documents when you can hear and speak the language," Dan said. "But I imagine without support, Deaf clients feel how I'd feel walking into a room in Mexico without speaking Spanish."

Dan said it'd take a lot to instill security, trust, and ease of mind in a situation like that, especially around something as serious as buying property. So, he enjoys that when we work together, we can achieve that for Deaf and HoH clients.

"When they walk out of the closing room, they understand what they've signed because they had you and an interpreter by their side the whole time. I can tell it makes a difference through the expressions on their faces and how excited they are." That's the goal: creating an environment where people can *celebrate* life's milestones, rather than worry that they're missing something important.

Deaf and HoH Culture Insight: Finding a Real Estate Agent

Ever since I helped my parents buy their home when I was 12 years old, I've been passionate about helping Deaf and HoH buyers and sellers navigate this process. If you or someone you know needs a real estate agent, I'd love to provide support.

For those in Colorado and Florida: I'm licensed in your state and would love to help you buy a home that meets your needs. Visit https://GallucciHomes.com to learn more or get in touch.

For those in other states: I started a company called ASL Realty to help connect the Deaf and HoH community with accessible real estate services. Visit https://ASLrealty.com to find expert support in your area for buying or selling a home.

When Easy Communication Matters Most

Some of the biggest moments in adulthood happen under pressure like birth, grief, and change. And when everything is unfolding fast, the ability to communicate clearly becomes everything.

Rian's birth was scheduled. We were living in the mountains at the time, and the doctors didn't want me delivering at a high elevation. So, we drove down to Denver and checked into the hospital, ready to meet my second baby before the next snowstorm rolled in.

After I got situated in my hospital bed, my dad and I had a few minutes to chat before the big event. We signed back and forth as nurses shuffled around me, and Dad made a joke that the baby was already running late to his own birthday party. One of the nurses grinned and waved a hand at us.

"I'm Audrey," she signed toward us both. "Nice to meet you."

My nurse was not only fluent in ASL, but she was Deaf. My Dad and I beamed at each other, and I felt a wave of relief wash over me. Unlike all of those times I'd sat in hospital rooms interpreting for my mom during her battle with cancer, my family and I could speak directly with medical staff during a life-changing moment in the language that worked best for us.

Most Deaf or HoH families have to book an interpreter weeks out or rely on shaky VRI. I was already nervous about bringing a new baby into the world. Having someone I could communicate with in my native language—and could also interpret what was happening for my dad—was a huge relief.

Audrey stayed by my side and asked about my pain levels in ASL so I didn't have to speak. I understood the doctors around me, but signing how I felt brought more ease and comfort to the whole experience.

Welcoming Rian into the world was a blessing, and having Audrey felt like a generous gift I hadn't even thought to ask for. Between contractions, we got to talking about Rian's godmother, Teresa, and made a wild connection.

Teresa is from Ecuador. She came over as an exchange student when she was fifteen, and later we became good friends because she's involved with the Deaf and HoH community. I knew Teresa had learned ASL from the host family she stayed with back then, but I didn't know who that family was.

"You'll never believe this," Audrey signed. "That was my family Teresa stayed with during her exchange year!"

"No way," I signed. "What are the chances?"

Audrey stayed past her shift change to make sure Rian arrived safely, and I had everything I needed. Once he was settled into his bassinet, she made sure to share a message with him in ASL: "You are loved."

For most families, communication in your native language is a given in the delivery room. For mine, it was a gift. In moments like these when you're in pain, overwhelmed, and things happen fast, being able to express yourself easily is everything. Everyone deserves a beautiful birth story that isn't marred by communication challenges. It's on all of us to make sure those with communication differences have the support to enjoy once-in-a-lifetime experiences with as much presence and joy as anyone else.

One way hearing folks can do that is by learning some ASL. This language comes in handy in more ways than you'd think.

Just recently, my sister Melissa's best friend had a major stroke at 51 years old. She understands when you talk to her, but she still can't speak. My sister has started teaching her ASL to support her communication.

Even if you don't have a Deaf or HoH family member, you can help ensure people have access to the communication method that works best for them, so they can still take part in life's most meaningful moments.

Deaf & HoH Culture Insight: What If Your Baby Is Born Deaf?

Despite having two Deaf parents, my siblings and I were all born with perfect hearing, as were our children. But roughly 2 to 3 out of every 1,000 babies are born with some level of hearing loss. In over 90% of those cases, the parents are hearing.[4]

Most babies are screened for hearing loss before they go home from the hospital. However, not all types of hearing loss show up at birth. Like my mom, some children develop it later due to illness, injury, genetics, or gradual onset. Or it might not be caught until delays in speech or social development appear.

As we discussed in chapter 5, if your baby is diagnosed with any degree of hearing loss, the most important gift you can give them is early access to language. That might mean learning a signed language like ASL.

---

4 "Quick Statistics About Hearing," National Institute on Deafness and Other Communication Disorders, U.S. Department of Health and Human Services, September 20, 2024, https://www.nidcd.nih.gov/health/statistics/quick-statistics-hearing.

> Another gift you can give your child is helping them to connect with the beautiful culture they're now part of: the Deaf and HoH community! Many states have mentorship programs that connect families with Deaf adults.

Navigating Adulthood as a CODA

Life's most special moments—welcoming a baby, saying goodbye to someone we love, or even buying a house—are never just about the logistics. They're about the emotional stories that shape who we are and the people we share them with.

Whether you're cooking dinner in a Deaf-friendly home or toasting someone you love on their wedding day, communication is what makes it possible to be completely present. When language flows freely without confusion or delay, you get to focus on what matters: love, celebration, grief, laughter, and belonging.

My experience of adulthood as a CODA has allowed me to notice what gets missed when communication isn't accessible. While I often had to help fill in the gaps, the Deaf and HoH community has made the big moments in my life even more meaningful. This culture has given me a deeper sense of connection through language and shared experiences. This family has made the best parts of life that much sweeter.

As a CODA, I've seen what's possible when Deaf and HoH adults are met on their terms—and the opportunities that get missed when they're not. The world can learn a lot from those stories, so we'll dive into more in chapter 10.

Key Chapter Takeaways

- Deaf-friendly home designs can foster connection for any family. Open floor plans and visual access to shared spaces make communication easier, especially if using sign language. Keep this in mind to make spaces more inclusive.
- Communication access isn't optional. It's foundational to life's most important moments. Make sure to plan events like weddings and funerals with equal communication access for everyone who attends.
- Small efforts can have a significant impact. By learning a few signs, asking someone about their preferred communication method, or simply showing patience, you can help bridge gaps and foster meaningful connections.

Prompts for Deeper Reflection

1. Think back to a major life event you've experienced. Was everyone able to participate fully? What, if anything, might have made the moment more inclusive?
2. Have you ever hesitated to communicate with someone because you weren't sure how? What would it look like to approach that moment with curiosity and a willingness to learn instead?
3. What are a few signs that would be helpful for you to know in ASL in case someone who signs needs your support? Can you spend some time today looking them up and practicing?

CHAPTER 10

WHAT INCLUSION REALLY LOOKS LIKE

Rian and I were waiting for the train at Denver International Airport like we'd done a dozen times before. We weren't in a rush, so we stood chatting next to our luggage, until I noticed the man standing next to us looked lost. He glanced up at the signs, then back down at his phone. After he did that a few times, I leaned over to get his attention.

"Hey, do you need help? Where are you trying to go?"

He looked up at me and said, "I'm Deaf."

I smiled and repeated my question in ASL.

His eyes widened. "Oh," he signed. "You know sign language?"

"Yeah," I signed back. "Fluently. I'm a CODA."

From there, it was easy to help him figure out which train to take. After a few quick directions, he was on his way. But the interaction stuck with me. Even when we carry all of the information in the world on our phones, a simple moment of connection between two people still makes a difference.

At the airport that day, I was proud to be a CODA, but I still could have helped even if I didn't know ASL. It would have taken 30 seconds to write down my question or type it into my phone. My life has shown me that the world would be a better place if everyone were more willing to connect, and even if it feels unfamiliar at first, *just try* anyway.

I've spent much of this book telling stories from my perspective as a CODA: what it was like growing up in a Deaf family, navigating two cultures, interpreting as a kid, and learning to advocate for people who matter to me. I hope my stories and experiences have highlighted the power of connecting with people whose lives differ from our own.

But the truth is that even though I grew up in the Deaf and HoH community, I'm still a hearing person. I've had hearing privilege, the benefit of being fluent in ASL, and the ability to move between Deaf and hearing spaces and conversations with relative ease. Not everyone shares that reality. And even among CODAs, no two people experience this world the same way.

So, instead of focusing only on what I think would make the world more inclusive, I want to highlight more voices in the Deaf and HoH community. Since my parents are no longer here to share their own experiences, I reached out to Deaf and HoH friends, fellow CODAs, hearing spouses, and others within this community to learn what inclusion looks like in their everyday lives, what they think society gets right, and what they wish more people knew.

When Small Gestures Make a Big Difference

Inclusion is often about the small things. It's in the daily interactions that either make someone feel welcome or excluded. Take something as routine as going to the store. If a Deaf or HoH person needs help finding something, pointing in a vague direction might not be enough. If a hearing person needs help and realizes the person they're asking is Deaf or HoH, speaking louder or mouthing the words usually isn't effective. So, what should you do?

Gella, a friend who is Deaf, told me about a time when she couldn't understand what another customer was saying to her at the grocery store. After Gella told her she was Deaf, the woman gently gestured to a two-liter bottle of soda on a high shelf.

"How many do you need?" Gella asked after handing over the first bottle.

The lady put up two fingers, so Gella grabbed another for her.

This interaction may sound ordinary to some, but these everyday moments can help someone feel seen. You'd be surprised by how many stories I've heard from the Deaf and HoH community that don't go as smoothly as Gella's interaction. Imagine a stranger asks you a question, you tell them you're Deaf, their face goes blank, and they walk away as if you're suddenly invisible. It happens more than you'd think, even when there are simple ways to approach the situation with kindness.

Gella says she loves it when people come up with gestures to communicate with her. Even if they don't know ASL, visual cues are the most helpful approach for her, like putting two fingers up to indicate "two bottles." She says mouthing words creates more challenges. Things can get lost in translation, and that turns what should have been a quick moment of connection between strangers into something awkward and frustrating.

It's worth looking beyond what you *think* you know about someone's situation and instead paying attention to the person standing in front of you. Presence is such a simple yet meaningful show of respect.

Sean, the hearing husband of Nadelle (my good friend who is Deaf), once said something to me that sums this up perfectly: "When a customer service rep answers Nadelle's question while looking her in the eye, it makes me feel like they get it. They understand how much it means to really see the person in front of you."

"Even better, though," he said, "is when they actually sign the answer. That's a tell-the-manager-they-deserve-a-bonus moment!"

Speaking to an interpreter or hearing family member instead of the Deaf or HoH person in front of you can feel like you don't fully *see* them. You don't have to know the other person's language to show you care about connecting with them, even if that connection looks a little different from what you're used to.

> ## Communication Tip: A Different Way to Think About Disability
>
> Did you know there are different models for how we can think about disability? This topic could be its own book, but here are the basics:
>
> **The medical model of disability** focuses on what a person can't do. It views disability as a problem that exists within the individual, like something to fix, cure, or work around.
>
> **The social model of disability** says that people aren't disabled by their bodies. Instead, they're disabled by the limitations of our society. Under this model, someone who's Deaf or HoH isn't "missing" anything. They're only excluded when communication isn't made accessible.
>
> Try to view communication differences and disabilities through the social model of disability. This helps shift the focus from pity to possibility. With this lens, the conversation isn't *What's wrong with you?* Instead, it becomes: *How can we make this world better for everyone?*

Different Worlds, Shared Truths

One perspective that stood out to me came from Cliff Moers, the former director of the Colorado Commission for the Deaf, Hard of Hearing, and DeafBlind. Cliff is Deaf, but his experience differs from many of the Deaf and HoH people I've talked about so far. He comes from a multigenerational Deaf family—his parents, grandparents, and siblings are all Deaf, too.

Since Cliff grew up in a Deaf household and was deeply immersed in the tight-knit Deaf community, he felt included through the shared experiences and rich visual language of ASL that he shared with the people around him.

"In this way," Cliff told me, "being Deaf is not unlike being part of an ethnic minority. We share a culture, a way of understanding the world, and a deep sense of belonging."

He remembers seeing non-Deaf people as different from himself and his family. But watching his parents carry a notepad and pen everywhere to communicate with hearing people reminded him that his family's way of life wasn't always understood. He went from seeing Deafness as his norm to realizing it can be invisible until someone realizes he moves through the world differently.

He said, "Over time, I've come to understand that many people may never truly grasp what it means to be Deaf, and that people from all walks of life are more alike than not. Some still pity us or view our way of life as something that needs to be fixed."

Cliff also pointed out something that made me stop and think: "Many who strongly *oppose* gender transition often *support* the use of DNA engineering or cochlear implants to 'convert' deaf infants and toddlers into hearing children, when we exist for a reason."

He brought up an important point. Somehow, altering a Deaf child's identity so they assimilate better with the hearing world is seen by many as acceptable because it moves them closer to what society considers "normal." Yet, affirming someone's identity in areas like gender is often treated as controversial or even unacceptable. The contradiction is telling: Society tends to support changing a person when it makes them more comfortable to be around, not when it makes that person more comfortable in *themselves*.

Cliff said, "I often wonder why the world struggles so much to live in harmony and simply respect people for who they are when we are all human beings. There's no shame in being Deaf. There's beauty in it—profound, complex beauty that reflects the diversity of the world we live in. It is a part of my identity that I cherish, and I hope others can begin to see it not as a limitation but as a perspective worth understanding and celebrating."

Inclusion looks different for everyone but it doesn't mean changing people to fit the world. Instead, it's about changing the world to better embrace people as they are. Try to see the beauty in people's differences and meet them with patience rather than uneasiness. While we may not always share the same experiences, we all know how much better it feels to be accepted.

A Little Empathy Goes a Long Way

My friend Debbie's mom is Deaf in one ear and has a speech impediment. I asked her what she wished hearing people knew about communicating with the Deaf and HoH community in everyday life.

She didn't hesitate: "Be patient! They are far more frustrated than you."

It's something we don't think about often enough as hearing people. We get annoyed when we have to repeat ourselves and assume the other person wasn't paying attention. But imagine how frustrating it must be as someone with hearing loss to have to ask people to repeat themselves *again*, knowing the hearing person is losing patience.

Debbie told me that when people get impatient, her mom starts pretending she heard what was said even when she didn't. She gets embarrassed and just wants to be included, so she smiles and nods even when she's secretly still left out.

When people don't make the effort to empathize, their reaction to unfamiliarity can escalate into something more painful. Debbie also told me that people used to make fun of her mom. Sometimes it was thoughtless curiosity. Other times, it crossed into outright cruelty. She remembers the sting of questions like:

"Is your mom from another country?"

"Why does she talk funny?"

"Why does she have a lisp?"

"Don't you hear the way she sounds?"

"What's wrong with her?"

Debbie still remembers those questions because what we don't know about someone else's experience isn't always benign. We can lean in with genuine curiosity and kindness, rather than turning someone's difference into a spectacle or a punchline. A better approach might be to simply ask, "What's the most supportive way to communicate with your mom?"

Meeting people where they are, without assumptions or impatience, is a basic act of kindness, but it also benefits *you*. The Deaf and HoH people in my life are such incredible friends. They're so expressive and funny. They make you feel included and care deeply about showing up for you.

When I'm with this community, I laugh harder and feel more loved and accepted than anywhere else. This is the kind of connection we miss out on when we don't take time to learn about each other. Individuals, businesses, and society as a whole could gain a lot by slowing down to find out what's actually helpful for those with communication differences. Try approaching life that way and watch how your world becomes better for it, too.

> **Fun Fact: The Deaf Goodbye**
>
> One thing I love about the Deaf and HoH culture is that saying goodbye takes a while. (And I'm Italian, so add even more time to that!)
>
> That's because communication is layered and communal. People are often deep in multiple conversations at once, and when one winds down, another picks up. You also don't just say goodbye to the host. You say goodbye to everyone.
>
> For CODAs and Deaf families, this is just part of life. We know that when the lights come on or the event is winding down, we have at least another 30 to 45 minutes before we actually leave.
>
> As a kid, I'd tug at my mom's shirt and ask to go home. But now I see it as a meaningful part of the culture—a way of assuring everyone is truly seen by everyone else before we part ways.

Equal Access Isn't Optional

As individuals, there's a lot we can do to help people feel included. But inclusion is also about how we design public spaces. Think about your experience going to a movie or live performance. If you're hearing, you just buy a ticket and show up.

But if you're Deaf or HoH, it might not be so simple. Every time I went to the movies with my parents, we had to ask the same question at the ticket booth: "Is this showing accessible?"

More often than not, the person behind the register didn't

know what to do with us. A few times they even offered to turn the volume up. Of course, that wouldn't help my parents at all.

One time, we were told the movie had closed captions, so we bought tickets for the whole family and settled in just as the trailers started. But the captions never appeared. I went to the front desk to ask what was going on, and the staff eventually admitted the captioning system was broken.

That meant my whole family, popcorn in hand, had to get up and leave the theater.

Accessibility can make the difference between being part of the experience or being shut out of it. The lack of working captions that day was enough to turn a fun family outing into a frustrating one.

Things are improving. Many theaters now have CaptiView devices that sit in your cup holder and display captions in real time. Some theaters offer open caption showings where the captions are built right into the film so everyone sees them. But the lack of accessibility still happens more often than you'd think—and not just at the movies.

One of my friends who is Deaf, Lori, told me about an issue she experiences often at public events: people ignore the seats reserved for Deaf and DeafBlind attendees.

Church services, concerts, and community fundraisers often have a limited number of seats reserved near the front of the stage so Deaf and DeafBlind guests can see or be near their interpreters. If you're in the Deaf or HoH community and rely on your vision to understand the world around you, not being able to see the interpreter's hands, face, and body language means you can't enjoy the show.

But Lori said she's shown up more than once to find those seats taken by people who don't rely on ASL to communicate. When Lori politely asks if they need to be able to see the interpreter, they usually admit that they don't.

Accessibility isn't "first come, first served," and it isn't optional. Treating it that way is exclusionary and can put people in uncomfortable situations.

Sean, Nadelle's hearing husband, actually learned ASL before meeting her so he could better communicate with his son, who is autistic. Sean told me about a small-town graduation he and his wife attended where his language skills got him roped into a role he hadn't signed up for. The event had no formal accommodations. But the people in charge of the event knew he could sign, so they assumed he could serve as the interpreter. They gave him interpreter seating without asking if he was comfortable interpreting—and without compensating him for it.

Sean said, "I was stuck doing something I'm not trained to do in front of hundreds of people."

He felt pressured to help as the only hearing person in the room who could sign, but knowing ASL doesn't automatically make you a qualified interpreter. It's unfair to expect Deaf and HoH people and their families to solve their own communication challenges at the drop of a hat.

No one should have to fight for access every time they step into a public space. All Deaf and HoH people deserve to feel proud of the culture they belong to and the unique ways they communicate—not embarrassed or left out or treated like they're inconveniencing others.

We'd all benefit from living in a world where more people are given the space and confidence to embrace who they are. When the right support is in place, something powerful happens: People feel free to show up fully as themselves. They embrace their talents and strengths with confidence. They make a loving and powerful stamp on the world.

Fun Fact: The Universal Appeal of Captions

Captions in TV shows and movies can add something special to the viewing experience for everyone.

Netflix's *Stranger Things* once went viral for its captions with visceral descriptions like "[tentacles squelching wetly]."

The goal was to make sure Deaf and HoH viewers could fully experience the eerie, sensory atmosphere of the show. But hearing audiences loved these vivid captions too, and suddenly an accessibility tool became part of the fun.

Not only are these captions way more entertaining than generic ones like "[soft music plays]" that don't contribute anything meaningful to the experience, but they're also a great example of how we all benefit when accommodations are done well.

When We All Belong, We All Win

My friend Melissa, who is hearing, told me about how inspiring it has been to watch her young daughter's journey with hearing loss.

Melissa told me, "From a young age, Deafness and hearing loss never fazed her, and still do not. Her confidence, resilience, and unwavering sense of self have taught me to find light in life's challenges and to see them not as limitations, but as opportunities for growth."

Her daughter was born HoH but went profoundly deaf after she'd learned how to speak. Melissa says her daughter has shown her how powerful it is when you're adaptable, confident, and content in who you are.

She continued, "My daughter faces each challenge as a puzzle to solve or a new path to explore. Her ability to say 'excuse me' or 'can you repeat that' without embarrassment or hesitation has shown me the true power of self-advocacy."

Melissa says her daughter seems to have this inherent belief that most people simply haven't been exposed to Deafness or hearing loss and just need a little perspective. I think she's right. Over the course of my life, I've seen that gaining perspective on other people's experiences has the power to change everything.

To me, an inclusive world is one where children like Melissa's daughter can grow into adults who still proudly take up space, ask for what they need, and embrace what makes them unique. Because when people feel safe to be fully themselves, we *all* get to live in a world that's kinder, richer, funnier, and more connected because of it.

Key Chapter Takeaways

- Gestures, a notepad, or simply being patient can go a long way in making someone feel seen and respected.
- Presence is an important facet of inclusion. Small acts, like facing someone when you talk to them or pausing long enough to learn how someone communicates best, can make a big difference.
- Inclusion benefits everyone. Our lives are richer, more connected, and even more entertaining when we make space at the table for everyone.

Prompts for Deeper Reflection

1. When have you witnessed or experienced a small moment of true inclusion? What made it meaningful?
2. Are there places in your everyday life (like your workplace, home, or social events) where accessibility could be improved? What could you change?
3. When have you assumed someone's needs instead of asking them? How might that moment have gone differently if you'd paused to connect or listen first?

CONCLUSION

"Look, we all fit here!" my granddaughter, Niko, shouted.

We finally found a clearing on the sidewalk big enough for my whole family to stand and watch this year's Pride parade. We got ourselves situated just in time for the action to start.

The first floats started passing us and with them came a roar of music my dad would have loved, the kind so loud you can feel it in your chest. Rainbow flags rippled through the air. Beautiful people from all walks of life passed by dancing, and we all joined in. Bubbles and neon confetti made the air sparkle, and all at once I was reminded of why I love celebrating Pride.

This is an event where everyone accepts each other without judgment. No one has to hide who they are. It's a celebration, yes, but it's also deeply meaningful to so many people for so many reasons.

Unless you know what it's like to feel like an outsider or see someone else go through that firsthand, you can't realize how much being included can improve someone's internal world.

I looked down the row of my family laughing, dancing, and signing to each other over the noise. I smiled at my son Rian who had brought me to my first Pride parade several years before. Then I looked at my daughter Jordan and her children. They wore Pride shirts I picked out for them with "Be Kind" written on the front.

I thought to myself, *I'm so proud to have a family that lives out the values my parents taught us growing up. Kindness, connection, and showing up to celebrate each other exactly as we are.*

After the parade, we headed to Rian's house for Spaghetti Sunday—another tradition we've carried on from childhood. Rian turned up some music on his kitchen speaker and the party continued. I was immediately transported back to a loud family dinner with my parents in our childhood home.

Shoes piled up by the front door. Kids took off chasing each other around the couch. People banged on tables and signed to each other from across the room because we couldn't hear over all the chaos. I watched Jordan stir the sauce like I used to with one hand on the spoon and the other hand catching a kid. And for a second, I saw my mom in her.

My parents weren't there, but they *were*: in the language flying across the room, in the laughter, and in the way no one had to pretend to understand. It was a day all about including and *celebrating* one another for how we each show up in this world.

Our family isn't perfect, but that was never the goal. We learned how to be present from my parents. Being there for each other, even when our lives are totally different. Showing up and trying.

Love isn't about knowing everything or always getting it right. Like I told Chris before he met my dad for the first time: put your expectations aside and *just try.*

That's what I hope you take away from this book. It's not about aiming for perfection, but about trying your best and taking action where you can. Small efforts—reaching out instead of turning away, pausing to consider someone else's experience, and helping them feel welcome in a room where they're silently feeling left out—can change a person's life.

Because behind any label—Deaf, blind, queer, trans, disabled—is a human with feelings, stories, and brilliance that the world too often overlooks. When we slow down and meet people where they are, we are all better off.

As a CODA, I grew up bridging the gap between my Deaf parents and the hearing world. You can be a bridge too. You can make sure people see your face when you're speaking to them. You can ask what someone needs rather than assuming. You can say, "I'm not sure, but I'll try."

If you're wondering where to start, here are a few suggestions:

- **Share this book.** The more we share, the more people understand.
- **Show up in your community.** Inclusion starts where you are.
- **Educate others.** Use what you've learned to spark better conversations.

- **Join or support organizations** that fight for accessibility and rights.
- **Learn ASL or fund interpreter services** so more people can participate fully.

Inclusion and acceptance can live in your everyday actions. Let this book be your invitation to see others clearly and meet them with kindness. If you're ever unsure how to help, remember this:

Just try.

ACKNOWLEDGMENTS

Thank you to the Deaf, HoH, and CODA contributors, as well as the hearing friends, parents, interpreters, and advocates who so generously shared your stories. Your unique insights and experiences make this book richer and more complete, just as they do our community as a whole.

I never set out to speak *for* you. I wanted to write this book *with* you. With your support, I hope I've done that with the love and respect I've always received from the Deaf and HoH community.

To my family: Thank you for being the heart behind every story. This book wouldn't exist without my dad, mom, and bonus mom, Dixie, who raised me to see the good in the world and approach others with love and empathy.

Thank you to my siblings Ben, Urs, Chris, Melissa, and Rose for helping me navigate our CODA childhood and for encouraging me as I brought our shared memories to life on these pages.

Thank you to Jordan, Rian, and Chris for your patience, your belief in me, and for reminding me every day why these stories matter.

To my teams at Uptown Realty Group, Gallucci Homes, and Compass, and to everyone who believed this book needed to exist. Thank you for cheering me on while I balanced real estate and writing.

Thank you to With Heart Coaching, whose guidance and support in my business helped make space for this book to take shape.

A special thank you to my good friend Nadelle who walked beside me through the writing process and made sure this book honored our community with the care and integrity it deserves.

And to you, the reader, whether you're Deaf, HoH, a CODA, a parent, an educator, or simply someone trying to connect better with the people around you: thank you. I hope this book helps you show up for others, love more fully, and recognize the deep connection that's possible for all of us even if we communicate differently.

RESOURCES

There's always more to learn about the Deaf and HoH community. Below, I've given you a starting point, whether you're part of the community and looking for support with employment or home buying, you're a hearing person eager to learn ASL, or you just want to be more inclusive in everyday life. Explore these resources and share them with your community.

Learn More About Deaf Culture & Community

- **National Association of the Deaf (NAD)**: www.nad.org
  This national civil rights organization is dedicated to protecting the rights and access of Deaf and HoH people.
- **Deaf DOVE**: www.DeafDove.org
  Deaf Overcoming Violence through Empowerment offers advocacy, community education, and other services for Deaf and HoH survivors of abuse.
- **Colorado Association of the Deaf (CAD)**: www.cadeaf.org
  CAD provides local advocacy and resources for Deaf and HoH Coloradans.

Learn ASL

- **Start ASL**: www.StartASL.com
  This is a beginner-friendly online resource for learning ASL at your own pace.
- **Signing Savvy**: www.SigningSavvy.com
  Visit Signing Savvy for a searchable sign language dictionary with video demonstrations.
- **Language First**: https://language1st.org
  Language First provides support and advocacy for early ASL access to prevent language deprivation.
- **Lingvano**: https://www.lingvano.com/asl/
  Lingvano is an ASL learning app with video-based lessons. It's great for beginners.

Home Buying Support for the Deaf and HoH Community

- **ASL Realty**: www.ASLrealty.com
  This is the national platform I founded to connect Deaf and HoH clients with real estate agents who communicate in American Sign Language.

- **Gallucci Homes**: https://GallucciHomes.com/
  We help homebuyers from all walks of life in Colorado and Florida, with a special focus on fluent ASL real estate services for the Deaf and HoH community and support for the LGBTQ+ community.

- **ASL Compass Affinity Group**
  ASL Compass Affinity Group is a support system I founded to help home buyers within the Deaf and HoH community find real estate agents who can communicate in ASL in different areas across the US.

To find out more, please visit www.ASLRealty.com and get in touch via the contact form.

Employment Support for the Deaf and HoH Community

- **Job Accommodation Network (JAN)**: www.AskJan.org
  You'll find practical tips for inclusive hiring, workplace accommodations, and ADA compliance here.

- **National Deaf Center**: www.NationalDeafCenter.org
  The National Deaf Center offers data, research, and resources that support Deaf and HoH success in continuing education and training.

- **State Vocational Rehabilitation Programs**:
  Rehabilitation Services Administration
  These programs provide the Deaf and HoH community and people with disabilities support for pursuing employment. They are available in every US state.

Technology & Tools

Apps for Real-Time Communication:
- **Ava**: https://www.ava.me/
  Live captions for group conversations

- **Cardzilla**: http://www.cardzilla.ws
  Display messages in large text for easier communication in writing

- **Sorenson VRS**: https://sorenson.com/vrs/
  Video Relay Service for phone calls in ASL

- **Google Live Transcribe**
  Real-time captioning using voice recognition

Image used with permission.
Credit to iStock / Sabel Skaya.

GLOSSARY

Deaf and Hard of Hearing Culture

- **Audism**: The belief that hearing people are superior to Deaf people.
- **CODA (Child of Deaf Adults)**: Someone raised by one or more Deaf caregivers, like my siblings and me. CODAs often grow up bilingual and bicultural, navigating both Deaf and hearing worlds.
- **Deaf (capital D)**: Refers to the cultural identity of being Deaf. Deaf culture is as rich as any other with shared values, norms, traditions, and a primary language, like ASL.
- **deaf (lowercase d)**: Refers to the physical condition of hearing loss. This is often used in medical or clinical contexts.
- **Deaf and Hard of Hearing community**: Refers to the community affected by varying degrees of hearing loss, and the culture they share. This community is sometimes referred to with the shorthand DHH.
- **DeafBlind**: Individuals with both hearing and vision loss. DeafBlind individuals may use tactile signing, signing in their conversation partner's hands, to communicate.
- **Deaf Gain**: The idea that being Deaf offers gifts (community, culture, identity, language, connections,

and more) rather than being a "loss" or something to fix.

- **Deaf+ (Deaf Plus)**: Someone who is Deaf or HoH and also has one or more additional disabilities.
- **Hard of Hearing (HoH)**: Individuals with partial hearing loss who may use speech, sign, or both.
- **Hearing Privilege**: Societal advantages held by hearing people, often unrecognized, that the Deaf and HoH community don't have.
- **Mainstreaming**: Placing Deaf students in general education classes, often without proper access to communication or support.
- **Name Sign**: A culturally given name in ASL that's used instead of fingerspelling every letter of a person's written name.

Language & Communication

- **ASL (American Sign Language)**: A full visual language with its own grammar and structure, used by the Deaf community in the US.
- **BSL (British Sign Language)**: A signed language used in the UK. It's completely different from ASL, despite the UK and the US sharing the common language of English.
- **Code-switching**: Shifting between languages or behaviors depending on context, like my siblings and I do sometimes between ASL and spoken English.
- **Cued Speech**: A visual system that uses hand shapes and positions near the mouth to make spoken language easier to lipread.

- **Fingerspelling**: Spelling words letter-by-letter using the ASL alphabet.
- **Language Deprivation**: When a child lacks access to a first language early in life. For Deaf and HoH children, this can be due to delayed or denied exposure to a signed language like ASL.
- **Lipreading**: Watching mouth movements to understand speech.
- **Pidgin Signed English (PSE)**: A blend of ASL signs and English word order that's more flexible than SEE. Many Deaf adults don't use "pure" ASL all the time. It's more common to see PSE in daily conversation or classrooms.
- **Signing Exact English (SEE)**: A sign system that follows English grammar and word order more closely than ASL.
- **Tactile Signing**: Signing into someone's hands for DeafBlind communication.

Access & Accommodations

- **Assistive Listening Devices**: FM systems, hearing loops, or amplifiers that help transmit sound in classrooms or public spaces.
- **Closed Captions (CC)**: On-screen text that shows both dialogue and sound cues.
- **Cochlear Implants**: A surgically-implanted electronic device that stimulates the auditory nerve to help people with hearing loss regain hearing.
- **Interpreter**: A professional who facilitates communication between two languages, like spoken

English and ASL. Interpreters are expected to be neutral, trained professionals, not family members or friends.

- **Non-ASL Interpreters**: Interpreters who use other modes of communication, like spoken English support, SEE, or another signed language.
- **Note Takers**: Trained staff or responsible students who type or write real-time summaries or transcripts of what's being said in a class or meeting.
- **Oral Transliterators**: People who silently mouth what's being said so a Deaf or HoH person can lipread more easily, often from a close visual range.

ABOUT THE AUTHOR

Maria Gallucci is a multi-award-winning real estate agent, a proud CODA (Child of Deaf Adults), and a lifelong advocate for inclusive communication. Growing up as one of six hearing children raised by Deaf parents, Maria learned American Sign Language before English and acted as an unofficial interpreter, helping her parents buy a home when she was 12 years old. Her childhood shaped her passion for helping people feel seen and respected, especially those who are often overlooked or misunderstood.

For more than 30 years, Maria has supported homebuyers from all walks of life with a special focus on serving the Deaf, Hard of Hearing, and LGBTQ+ communities. She's the founder of Uptown Realty Group and Gallucci Homes, a top-producing agent at Compass Real Estate, and among the top 1.5% of agents nationwide. She also founded ASL @ Compass Affinity group and ASL Realty, a national platform connecting Deaf and Hard of Hearing clients with agents who communicate in American Sign Language.

Outside of real estate, Maria serves on the boards of the Rocky Mountain Deaf School, DOVE (Deaf Overcoming Violence through Empowerment), and CAD (Colorado Association of the Deaf). She's passionate about language access, cultural inclusion, and creating spaces where everyone truly belongs.

Maria's motto—*just try*—is a reminder that meaningful connection can start with one small step. You don't have to be perfect to communicate with someone who's different from you. You don't even have to speak their language. You just need to be willing to try.

Raised in Silence is Maria's first book, a love letter to the community that brought her up and a guide for anyone seeking to bridge communication gaps in their own life.

Gallucci Homes

galluccihomes.com | @galluccihomes

ASL Realty

aslrealty.com | @asl.realty

www.ingramcontent.com/pod-product-compliance
Lightning Source LLC
Chambersburg PA
CBHW061754120626
46550CB00005B/1989